AN UNLIKELY
PROPHET

AN UNLIKELY PROPHET

A METAPHYSICAL MEMOIR BY THE LEGENDARY WRITER OF SUPERMAN AND BATMAN

ALVIN SCHWARTZ

Destiny Books
Rochester, Vermont

Destiny Books
One Park Street
Rochester, Vermont 05767
www.DestinyBooks.com

Destiny Books is a division of Inner Traditions International

Library of Congress Cataloging-in-Publication Data
Schwartz, Alvin, 1916–
   An unlikely prophet : a metaphysical memoir by the legendary writer of
Superman and Batman / Alvin Schwartz.
      p. cm.
   "Originally published in 1997 by MacMurray & Beck under the title
An unlikely prophet : revelations on the path without form."
   Summary: "A profound investigation into the shifting nature of identity and
reality"—Provided by publisher.
   Includes bibliographical references.
   ISBN 1-59477-108-1 (pbk.)
   1. Superman. 2. Spiritual life. 3. Cartoonists. 4. Buddhism. I. Title.
PS3569.C5649U55 2006
   813'.54—dc22
                                                              2006004243

Printed and bound in the United States by Lake Book Manufacturing, Inc.

10 9 8 7 6 5 4 3 2 1

Text design by Ginny Scott-Bowman and text layout by Jon Desautels
This book was typeset in Sabon with Agenda as the display typeface

For Rich Morrissey

We must take on our existence as broadly as we possibly can; everything, even the unheard of, must be possible in it. This, underneath all, is the only courage that is demanded of us: to have courage for the most strange, the most inexplicable.

—RAINER MARIA RILKE

Chapter One

t truly does come. I believe it actually presents itself over and again, though few recognize it as it struggles to thrust through the screen of "rationality." But I now know that to everyone at some crucial time comes an opportunity to become aware of a greater reality and a greater freedom. In my case it came late, with a bewildering leap into the unknown.

It was spring of 1994—not very long ago in time but eons ago in terms of experience. I got this strange call late in the afternoon.

"Are you the Superman writer?"

Ah, I figured. One of those. Another comics fan. Thirty-five years ago, when I was still writing the stuff, no one ever called me. Today, how things have changed. Yesterday's literary drudges among the ranks of comics writers have gradually become luminaries. And the Golden Age survivors like myself are especially sought out by thousands of fans—not just kids but nostalgic baby boomers with a strong preference for the kinds of stories that were done during their own childhoods. In 1994 my old Batman newspaper strips from the 1960s had recently been reprinted in deluxe editions

—bringing unexpected emoluments in the form of both cash and requests for public appearances.

"Are you the Superman writer?" the voice repeated into my hesitant silence.

"Yes, I am."

"And Batman? You wrote Batman too?"

"Yes, Batman too." There was something about the voice I couldn't place. An odd accent with nasal resonances lifting the vowels into prominence from an unmistakable base of Oxonian English. Possibly Oriental, but I'd never heard anything quite like it before.

"I have a great need to see you."

"I don't know that that's possible right now."

"It's a question of great necessity. Do not put me off, Mr. Schwartz, when you are the only one who can understand."

From time to time I come up against some real nuts. But in some odd way, this didn't sound like one of them. So instead of putting him off, I asked, "Understand what?"

"Recently you gave a lecture on Superman at the University of Connecticut, yes?"

"Well—about five years ago."

"And subsequently the lecture was printed in a learned journal called *Children's Literature*?"

"That's true. Only it came out about three years ago."

"Let's not fuss about time, Mr. Schwartz. In that lecture you treated Superman in a very special way, did you not?"

"I'm not sure what you mean."

"As though he were alive and not merely a creature of the imagination. Surely you remember that?"

"Oh—you mean where I said something about how we writers and editors didn't fully realize that we had been taken over by him?"

"That he had a life of his own—quite so. A most striking insight."

"But that was just a conceit. I didn't mean it literally."

"You had to have meant it, Mr. Schwartz. It's the basis of your whole lecture. You must not back away from so keen an insight, even though there may be pressures—"

"Come on! What pressures? It was just a fanciful way of describing my experience. Now, if you'll excuse me, my friend, I have to—"

"No—no—don't dismiss me like that. You're my best hope. Since I happen to be in a similar state. You see?"

"What similar state?"

"Like Superman."

I fell silent, convinced finally that I had a genuine spinach head on the other end of the line.

Into my silence the caller announced urgently, "I am not crazy, sir. Like the Superman you describe in your lecture, I am an idea become real. And you are the only one I have encountered in years who seems capable of grasping such a possibility."

"Yes—well—that's all very interesting. I'd like to discuss it further with you. But you caught me at a bad time. I've got someone at the door right now. But—feel free to contact me again. Write me. Put it in a letter. Okay? So good-bye for now." And I hung up.

I thought that was the end of it. As it turned out, it was only the beginning.

He showed up at my door about two days later.

My wife and I have this big, rambling house in northern Westchester. It's gotten even bigger since the kids moved out to set up homes of their own, but we kind of like having all that space to rattle around in. It isn't empty space, anyway. Every nook and cranny is a reminder of a bit of family history, and even though it's a lot harder for us to take care of than when we were young, we haven't yet gotten around to accepting that fact, though many years have passed since I remarried and not long after quit Detective Comics over conflicting visions of Superman.

In 1989 my oldest son was running an ad agency in Montreal,

and one of his clients was a large children's book publisher, which led him to take a summer course in children's literature. It was being given at Concordia University in Montreal by a visiting professor from the University of Connecticut who had earned quite a reputation by transforming a subject once disdainfully referred to in English departments as "kid lit" into a field of serious academic interest. My son happened to mention in class one day that his father used to write Superman. That resulted in an immediate invitation to me to come talk to the class, which my son made an imperative. I showed up, I spoke, I answered questions, and everyone, it seemed, enjoyed it, including me. So when Dr. Francelia Butler invited me to lecture the following fall to her regular class at UConn, with no strictures on my self-assumed role as cultural anthropologist, I was glad to do so.

My talk went well and subsequently appeared in the journal *Children's Literature,* founded and edited by Dr. Butler. I gave it the title "The Real Secret of Superman's Identity." The conceit I used to develop my theme, that Superman acquired a kind of reality that controlled his writers and editors without their realizing it, had excited the mysterious caller enough to seek me out. Let me quote from the opening paragraphs.

For about sixteen years, from the beginning of the forties to the mid-fifties, I suffered a peculiar kind of occupational thralldom. But I wasn't entirely aware of it. In fairy tales and legends, there are numerous stories of humans bound into the service of trolls, giants, witches and other demonic and supra-human entities. But in today's rational world, we are scarcely likely to recognize or give credence to such creatures. Consequently, when we are, in a very direct sense, taken over by such a being, we either tend to reduce it to mere psychology or deny that it's happening altogether.

In my case, as well as that of all my co-workers, we chose the path of denial. It simply never would have occurred to us that we were, to put it bluntly, "being directed." . . . I was not to understand until long afterwards, however, that it wasn't I, or any of the other writers or the editors . . . who directed Superman's destinies. Superman directed his own destinies. All of us were merely his pawns. But the realization seems to be, long after the fact, mine alone.

Of course, what I was trying to express was the fact that in the excitement of plotting, those of us involved in constantly thinking up new problems and situations to keep Superman going often spoke of him as a real person. We didn't have a compendium of his abilities. But we did have a sense of whether a certain application of his superpowers fitted his nature. In my case, of course, I had a very special feeling about that. You see, I and my editors knew Superman as a result of long hours spent worrying over him—the way you know an eccentric uncle after years of experience with his ways. So we couldn't tell a new writer exactly what Superman could do, or should do, or wouldn't do. It was necessary first to get acquainted with the character and develop a sense of him as we had. As though, in fact, he were really our living and independent eccentric uncle. Obviously the strange man on the phone didn't think, as I claimed, that this way of putting it was merely a conceit. And he was convinced I understood more than I was willing to admit, especially about the powers of the imagination.

To get to our home in northern Westchester without a car is virtually impossible. At least that's what I thought until my caller came pedaling up our long gravel driveway on an old bicycle and knocked at the side door leading into the kitchen. I was having a coffee and had seen him coming, a tall, ungainly man with a face mostly hidden in the hood of a long, loosely buttoned raglan garment that fell below his knees so that it flapped loosely around him and whose obvious wind resistance must have made cycling extremely difficult. At that moment I had no idea who he was, of course, but assumed, since he was bicycling, that he was from the neighborhood. When I went to answer his knock, I found myself looking up into the narrow, flat face of a man nearly seven feet tall who looked distinctly Oriental.

"How can I help you?"

"In many ways," was his unexpected reply. "I am Mr. Thongden."

And then I placed him, even though he hadn't given me his name when he'd phoned. I recognized the accent. I'd never heard anything quite like it before.

I remained in the open doorway, feeling a little unneighborly for hesitating to invite him in. "I had no idea you were from around here," I said. "I don't remember ever seeing you before."

"You have not," he said. "But we have spoken."

"Two days ago," I acknowledged. "But you didn't say you were local," I added, looking at the bike, which he balanced with two long fingers poised on the handlebars.

"Within bicycle range," he acknowledged with a sudden flash of teeth as he presented me with a smile. "Thirty-seven miles."

"You came thirty-seven miles to see me—on that?"

"It was necessary, since I came from New York." Again that swift, almost refractory smile.

I had a vision of him laboriously pedaling his way amid the coursing traffic on the Taconic State Parkway, the startled drivers slowing to stare at the grotesque apparition formed by his great height draped in that shapeless anorak as it fluttered and twisted in the wind. He must have come up by way of Tarrytown—Ichabod Crane on a bicycle.

"You must be tired," I said in sudden realization, opening the door a little wider, wordlessly inviting him inside despite my better judgment. I was alone in the house. Kay was off shopping at the Jefferson Mall over on Route 6.

He followed me into the kitchen and I offered to take his cloak. In a quick, lithe movement, startling in a man so tall, he slipped out of it and handed it to me. I hung it among other outdoor garments sharing a row of hooks alongside the door. Without so much as a by-your-leave he settled into the very seat I had occupied at the window when I spotted him coming up the driveway. My half-drained coffee cup rested in front of him. I moved it to the adjacent place, where I leaned over the back of a chair and watched him, not quite certain how to proceed with him.

"You said the name was—Thong—?"

"Thongden," he said. "The only one in the phone book."

I nodded. "Thongden," I repeated, somehow relieved that he was in the phone hook. "It's certainly an unusual name. Asian, of course?" The name kept jogging at my memory. I had this feeling I'd heard it before. But where? It was like a faint echo from long ago, elusive and vaguely discomfiting.

"Yes, but borrowed."

"You mean—it's not really your name?"

"I am basically nameless, but not without progenitors." He added, in response to my puzzled look, "We have much to talk about, Mr. Schwartz."

"I wouldn't be surprised," I admitted. I glanced down at the cold coffee in my cup. "Can I get you a coffee or something, Mr. Thongden?"

"Would tea be possible?"

"Certainly." I found the electric kettle on the sideboard and plugged it in. "I gather your coming here has something to do with—Superman?"

"Your version of him especially, as I already explained." As I spoke, he kept glancing over my left shoulder in a most disconcerting way.

"Because I spoke of him as a real person?"

"Because in thinking of him so, you made him real. Your own words."

"Not exactly," I said, wondering again whether I should have let him in.

The water was beginning to boil. "Would you like something with your tea? Sugar, milk?"

"Butter, perhaps?"

7

"Butter—in tea?"

"No one seems to like it here. But in Tibet, tea is almost always taken with butter. Yak butter, of course."

"Of course," I mumbled as though I remembered that everyone knew that. Then suddenly it struck me. "Tibet? You're from Tibet? But of course. Thongden is a Tibetan name, isn't it? I should have realized—"

"Yes, I am of Tibet. But not entirely."

I found a tea bag and dropped it into a large cup. "Anyway, we don't use butter. Saturated fat, you know? Will you take margarine instead?"

"No—just plain tea, thank you."

I poured the boiling water on top of the tea bag in the cup and placed it before him. "Tibet and where else?"

"It is not that simple, Mr. Schwartz. As with Superman, you can say in one sense that he is from the planet Krypton. But the Superman you describe as controlling you—he is not from Krypton." Again that puzzling glance of his over my left shoulder.

"Oh?"

"He is from you—from your imagination."

"I see. Actually, I didn't create Superman; Jerry Siegel and Joe Shuster did."

"No—no. They created the cartoon character. You created your personal living Superman."

I sat down and stared at him. "There's something I'm missing here."

"Of course," he said, grinning at me suddenly. "You didn't really, fully create Superman. But—you came close. And then you went on a long detour. But I am the one to put you back again on your path." He waggled a long finger at me. "As for myself, as you can see, I have been completely and thoroughly created."

I shook my head. "I'm afraid I don't see. I don't understand what you're getting at, Mr. Thongden."

"Why, simply that I'm real. You can touch me. You can have me as your guest, drinking tea with you at your table. And how that came to be is one of the things I'm here to discuss with you."

For the first time I began to have a premonition of where he was leading me. I didn't yet understand it. But I knew somehow that he wasn't crazy and that I was on the verge of confronting something truly confounding, "Then please discuss it, Mr. Thongden. How are you different from anyone else who might be visiting me over tea?"

"It is not easy to explain," Thongden confessed. "In Tibet, before the Chinese invasion, there would have been no problem. But here in the West, such things are not known, let alone believed in. Yet there are many like me, and have been many in the past, who have lived among you."

"Tell me."

"Do you know what a *tulpa* is?"

"A—what?"

"A t-u-l-p-a." He spelled it out so slowly and carefully that his long upper teeth showed behind his controlled lip movements. "*Tulpa,*" he repeated, speaking it with a soft, nasal sonority. A thin smile crossed his craggy features as he looked down at me. "A living human created by pure thought."

As he said this, I began to feel the hairs lifting at the back of my neck. But I slowly started remembering fragments of things I'd read long ago. "Is this the kind of thing—I mean—what certain Tibetan spiritual leaders—wise men—is this where they create a living being by—mind power?"

"Not only in Tibet, Mr. Schwartz. But anywhere in the world where the powers of the imagination are exercised."

"And you are—"

"A being created by the imagination of another man. A *tulpa,* as we're called in Tibet."

"Of course I don't believe a word of this," I said, sensing even as I said it that he was telling me the truth as he understood it, even though it was impossible. By now I was experiencing a tingling that spread across my back and up the surface of my skin to the top of my head. I could feel his presence as though I had suddenly come upon an unexpected shape late at night in a dimly lit room. Clearly Thongden wasn't like anyone else, at least not in the way I understood being human. "Are you telling me—" And then I broke off, unable to express what was on my mind.

"What, Mr. Schwartz?"

I looked at him, one finger thrust through the ear of his teacup as he held it near his mouth and stared at me across the rim. His eyes were a deep, translucent amber. He was wearing an old brown and gray wool sweater that had begun to unravel at the sleeves. From beneath its round neck emerged a striped, soft-collared shirt. It was open at the collar, and there seemed to be a place where either the neck itself faded into the shadows formed by the shirt, which was likely, or there was a hole, an emptiness where the flesh left off. But I assured myself that this image was simply my imagination getting out of hand.

"Are you telling me," I began again, "that you're—an apparition?" I heard the words come out of me and didn't fully believe I was uttering them.

Thongden responded with a short, plopping kind of laugh. "With a bicycle," he chortled. Again those depthless amber eyes confronted me. "I did not come into this world viviparously," he added, allowing a smile to hover on the full, flat features. "You, like most others, did. But that is a detail."

"Is it really?" was all I could think to say.

He got up from his seat as though to allow himself more room to wag a finger at me. "In the end, whatever the apparent means, we are all born of the imagination. 'Nothing ever existed that was not first imagined,' according to your English poet William Blake. But here in the West, unlike Tibet, you imagine matters differently." He tittered. "Do you have the least idea what I'm saying, Mr. Schwartz?"

Somehow he had ceased being fearsome to me. I was almost getting used to him. But he was extraordinary enough for me to wish Kay would return in time to see him for herself. I had no idea how I'd manage to describe him to someone else.

"No—you haven't the faintest idea. Yet there are those among you—" He switched his mode of explication suddenly. "Alexander Hamilton," he announced. "You know about him, don't you? You're an American."

"The first secretary of state," I said. "Founded the Federalist party. Might even have become president if he hadn't been killed in a duel. What about him?"

"Of uncertain parentage, we are told," Thongden continued. "An orphan who went on to achieve great things. Hah! There never were any parents, Mr. Schwartz. He simply turned up, Alexander Hamilton, whole and adult. The early personal history was mostly tagged on afterward. But I mention only one instance. There are others around today. But not so important."

"It's all a revelation to me," I said somewhat facetiously. I wasn't ready to acknowledge even to myself that he had me half believing his unbelievable claim. "Why do you come to me?"

"But you already know that."

"Because I suggested Superman was kind of a—a *tulpa*?"

"Because you had the vision to consider such a thing. I need someone like that. There aren't many, you know. You're a rare one in your own way, Mr. Schwartz. Yes—we have a special affinity for each other."

"We do?"

"You have a need for me. And I for you. But you are not aware yet of your own need. Which has to do, I may as well tell you, with working out your unique experience with Superman. You have to bring him back to life, you might say. But you cannot until you understand fully who and what he is to you. My need is much simpler. I need you to think about me."

"What do you mean?"

"You cannot spend fifteen years of your life concentrating on an archetypal figure like Superman and then walk away from it, leaving your relationship unresolved. I urge you to meditate on certain of your stories from the past and try to discover more of what you only hinted at in your article."

"Couldn't you be more specific?"

"At the right time. As for *my* need—I refer you again to Alexander Hamilton—you say he died in a duel. Not exactly. He knew he was fading away. The duel provided him with a simple way out. I am not ready to take a way out. Your need is too strong, you see. So if I am to show you the way, you must keep me going."

"By thinking about you," I repeated.

He was standing near the kitchen door now, removing his cloak from the hook and looking outside with an unexpectedly nervous air. "You won't be able to avoid it, for now," he announced. He chuckled, making a thin, dry noise in his throat as he drew the cloak over his shoulders, opened the door, and looked back at me. "Much food for thought," he said, and again he seemed to be looking over my shoulder.

"You're leaving? Just like that?"

"Only in appearance," he replied, repeating that dry, humorless chuckle. "But I shall be around. Sooner than you think. But for now, you need time to get your mind adjusted to this new factor in your life. And you need to better understand the presence that sits over your shoulder." He held up his hand with its long, spatulate thumb directed at the very spot where I thought I had seen him looking curiously at something when he first came in.

Involuntarily my hand rose and poised briefly just over my left shoulder. "What presence?"

"It's quite strong, considering," he said reflectively as he directed his amber gaze toward my left.

"What are you talking about?"

"Superman. Or perhaps more precisely, the Superman effect. It's still working on you after all these years." And then he was out the door.

I watched him walk outside, get on the bike, and start pedaling down the driveway. After he was out of sight I remained there at the table, staring out the window and futilely trying to tell myself that it could all have been some kind of weird waking dream. But if it had been such a dream, what a train of associations it brought with it. I started remembering things. One by one, other extraordinary events I had experienced over the years and conveniently forgotten started to come back to me. And I realized that each of them had happened after I had gotten involved with Superman, as though my Superman experience had provoked them or had somehow been an initiating factor.

Chapter Two

My writing Superman, or writing comics of any kind, would hardly have seemed a likely career path for me when I started out. I had no connection with the field and certainly no interest in it. Yet through a number of unexpected turns in the road, I somehow achieved what still strikes me as a kind of accidental celebrity through my supposedly significant role in helping create what historians of the medium call the Golden Age of Comics. That's a period that reaches back to the beginning of the '40s—actually a little earlier to allow room for that milestone in comics history, Jerry Siegel and Joe Shuster's Superman, which first appeared in DC's Action Comics in 1938. Accidental arrivals often disguise deeper currents and vital synchronicities, so it is, as I have now discovered, important to look closely at the paths that lead to them.

In 1938 I was twenty-two years old and had been the coeditor of a literary magazine called *Mosaic*, which I had started in high school and which had by then published work by many of the leading literary figures of the day, including Gertrude Stein, Ezra Pound, and William Carlos Williams. This was the direction I seemed to be going. And then in 1940 the road took its first unexpected twist.

It was the Depression. I was dickering with Duell, Sloan and Pierce to publish my first novel, and the prospects were beginning to dim. The title of that still unpublished work was *In Lasting Night,* and even if it had been published, I knew the meagerness of the advance would have left me financially "in lasting night" anyway. I did manage to sell the occasional magazine story through my then agent, Curtis Brown, but such sales were so few and far between that I couldn't count on them at all.

One day things got so bad I resorted to the desperate step that unexpectedly turned me into a comics writer. My wife and I had a small apartment on 8th Street in Greenwich Village. The rent had been unpaid for two mouths now, and food was decidedly low. However, since 8th Street was one of the busiest corridors in the Village, all I had to do was sit at my front window, looking down, and sooner or later someone I knew would come walking by and maybe lend me a quarter. In those days a quarter would buy a full Chinese dinner, complete with egg roll, soup, dessert, and fortune cookie.

The very first prospect who passed beneath my window on that fateful day was my friend Jack Small. Jack made a living drawing comics from scripts created by writers. Those scripts were similar to film scripts except that instead of describing what the camera was supposed to shoot, they described what the artist had to draw. They also provided the dialogue—much more difficult than film because too large a dialogue balloon stole room from the all-important picture. There were additional difficulties that made writing comics harder than writing film, but I was not to discover them until much later.

On that particular day in 1940, that is, two years after Siegel and Shuster's Superman made its successful debut in Action Comics, I ran down the steps of my Greenwich Village apartment, accosted Jack Small, and asked him if he could spare me a quarter.

Jack had a better idea. He knew I was a writer. Being an artist, he had no idea that being a writer was not in itself a qualification for writing comics. I didn't know it either, or maybe I wouldn't have tried. I didn't know that beyond writing ability, writing comics takes a certain kind of eidetic mind—that is, a special sense for images. It wasn't until some years later, when I was writing both the Superman and Batman newspaper strips, that I fully appreciated that it also takes a certain knack.

But I'm getting way ahead of my story.

"Look," Jack said on that seminal day, "I've been drawing a book called *Fairy Tale Parade*. And they're buying freelance stories, particularly Russian fairy tales. Why don't you give it a try?"

Jack arranged to get me a copy of a typical comic script to use as a pattern. I went to the library, found a Russian fairy tale I liked, adapted it, and turned it in to Jack's editor at the old Street and Smith Publishers Building, now taken over by Dell. DeGrouchy, the editor, told me their staff writer had just done the same story. "But," he said, "we'll have a look at it. If we like it, maybe we'll offer you another assignment."

That was that, I thought. But by the time I got home, there'd been a call from DeGrouchy, who told my wife that he liked my script better than their staffer's and was buying it, and would I please consider doing more of the same for him.

It began like that, in a small way.

A year later, at a Detective Comics Christmas party, to which my growing stature as a comics writer had earned me an invitation, the DC editors persuaded me to have a shot at Batman. It was a tough medium, requiring a kind of skilled plotting and a way of writing minimally. And then you also had to describe what each graphic was to contain—in detail. Like a movie scenario, but far more difficult.

My first Batman effort was so-so. But at least they assigned me another one. And another.

After my third Batman script, the editors really began to like my work. And I went on to write everything they threw at me. I wrote titles like "Vigilante," "The Flash," "Tomahawk," "Buzzy," "Date with Judy," "Slam Bradley," "Hayfoot Henry," "House of Mystery," "Hotel Skyline," "Aquaman," and even "Wonderwoman." And then one day they asked me to do Superman. At first I demurred, thinking the character somehow dull. When you're dealing with superpowers, I thought, what challenges can there be to make the character really interesting?

I remember that morning especially well, particularly what it was like as I left the office at Grand Central Palace—480 Lexington Avenue. That old address is as fresh in my mind after more than fifty years as was the feeling of spring even in the sludgy canyons of Lexington Avenue as I crossed the street to the little Chock Full o' Nuts sandwich shop, where I sat for an hour mulling over whether I should add Superman to all the other stuff to which I was committed. Odd how at such moments our perceptions can become sharpened and then shift to what at first appear to be details extraneous to the problem at hand. I noticed this very bland-looking, neatly dressed young man sitting at the counter directly across from me. I kept looking at him without quite understanding at first what intrigued me about him. He was probably one of the most ordinary-looking people I had ever seen. He was as vapid as the thin cheese-and-nut sandwich he was almost daintily munching on.

Sometimes we're thinking furiously and don't realize we're doing it. And then, abruptly, we become aware of ourselves, as I did at that particular moment when I suddenly made the connection with Superman's alter ego, Clark Kent. The thought came to me that there was something necessary about Clark's blandness—that it represented something universal, as though in the ordinariness of each of us there had to be a place of rest, of relief. I didn't yet grasp all the implications of this, except that Superman seemed to highlight that common condition because in him the extremes were so much greater—the ultra-powerful Man of Steel alongside the ultra-ordinary Clark Kent. The sharp contrast between the self as nonentity and the self as all-powerful seemed to suggest a secret, private, but universal experience.

I found myself fascinated by the complexities that seemed to lie hidden within the ordinariness of each of us. And that led me to recall some of the inexplicable gifts and capacities I had found in so many outwardly ordinary people. I remembered a musician who heard extraordinary Mozartian flashes of music in her head that she mostly never troubled to write down; a housewife who always knew when anyone in her large extended family was in trouble, no matter how far away the family member lived; one young man who worked at our local post office who could predict the weather several days in advance with virtual infallibility; a certain German refugee who had been too brutalized by the Nazis to hold a job anymore but who could walk into a betting parlor, make a modest wager, and never fail to walk away with enough to get him through a few days. Then there was Warden Day, a master lithographer who saw people's auras so that she always seemed to know their state of health and even their mood of the moment. Each of these "ordinary" people revealed greater or lesser kinds of "super" powers.

It's worth noting that these recollections were building up in me in a way that gradually became more personal. I didn't realize it back when it was happening, but after meeting Mr. Thongden I was somehow more sensitized to the way those early recollections brought me closer to myself as I sat in that sandwich shop trying to decide whether to add Superman to my commitments. As I circled about the decision that spring morning so many years ago, I found myself recalling a number of then recent anomalies in which I had participated, all of which occurred only a couple of years after I first started writing comics and which also made it possible for me to write and publish my first novel, *The Blowtop*. In doing that book I had unveiled something within me that would speak of things I didn't know I knew.

A few months after *The Blowtop* appeared, my artist wife and

I were visiting our near neighbors—Jackson Pollock, who was just beginning to make his major splash in the art world, and his wife, Lee Krassner, a fine painter as well. This was at Springs, East Hampton. With our homes facing each other from opposite sides of the small bay known as Accabonic Creek, we enjoyed enough friendly proximity and common interests to bring us together with some frequency. This was abetted by Jackson's belief that he had been the model for a major character in *The Blowtop,* which was only partially correct. But there was something different about this particular night as we all sat together in Pollock's living room.

My wife, Marjorie McKee, was avidly discussing ways of working, of uncovering that element in a canvas that went beyond what one knew. How did one get to it? Or more precisely, how did one awaken it?

"Let it uncover itself," Jackson said. "I just let it happen."

"But it doesn't just happen when you call on it," Marjorie said. "You have to prepare for it. You have to learn how to open yourself up."

"No," Jackson said. "That only gets in the way. You just let it happen. It's always there."

"I wish," I said, thinking both of my novels and my comic scripts, "that I could believe that. Sometimes when I'm working, it's there and it just flows along. Other times everything is just turned off. It's like trying to walk on hot bricks."

Jackson was never a heavy talker. He expressed himself very directly, almost monosyllabically. Now he stood up from his chair, towering over us. He was a tall man. "Come on, I'll show you."

We got up and followed him. I remembered how all three of us trooped to the adjoining studio, a roughly rebuilt barn alongside a house that did not as yet have central heating. There was quite a chill in the night air and a heavy redolence from the clam flats bordering Accabonic Creek. When Jackson switched the lights on, there, tacked down and spread out across most of the floor in the manner he had learned from Navajo sand painting, was one of those canvases whose gargantuan dimensions were also part of the Navajo style. I had seen Jackson's canvases stretched out like this before. I had even watched him at work on a couple of occasions. But there was something different in the air tonight. We were all somehow feeling more alert, more perceptive, and in an odd way more aware of each other. This particular canvas, which Jackson had begun earlier that day, was already partially covered with the squiggles that were characteristic of his work at the time. But of course they were not squiggles. There was an interesting pattern developing in this uncompleted work that I can only describe as a kind of variation on circles, as though the artist had been experimenting with an interplay of purely rolling motion, lines that became form through a process of acceleration, ceaseless, restless movement, cornerless and endless. At least, so it appeared to me.

But now Jackson was prying open a small can of house paint containing a color he rarely used at that time—one of the earth colors, a burnt umber. Holding the open can in one hand, he bent his tall, supple frame over the canvas and began to pour the paint out in long, running driblets. During all this, we remained absolutely silent. And I noticed something startling. I had seen Jackson do this before, but somehow I hadn't been as observant, perhaps because it wasn't something I was expecting to see. This time, though, my attention had been called to the process, and I began to realize that the paint did not seem to obey the law of gravity. It poured in impossible directions, never just straight down but splaying outward or sideways as though some other force were directing it. Jackson's hand was absolutely steady as he poured. He certainly was not overtly influencing the way the paint chose to drip. But then I realized that *the circular forms already on the canvas were doing the influencing* as though in their representation of pure acceleration they formed tiny gravitational fields of their own, tiny force fields that drew the paint in ways that corresponded to their various modes of motion. I thought of similar magic circles like Stonehenge and mandalas conjured by energies we had long forgotten and that modern physicists were only just beginning to skirt the edge of. Was this what Jackson meant by letting it happen? I asked after confessing I'd never noticed this effect before.

He shook his head. He had few words to explain it. "It's just always there. That's all I can say. I always do it."

"But why didn't I see it?"

Jackson shook his head. "No one ever does," he said.

I turned to Lee. "What do you think?"

"We usually just see what we expect to see," she replied. "The good stuff is always hidden back in the shadows where our expectations don't reach."

Maybe it had something to do with a kind of opening out because of the Pollock experience, but in any case, a few months later, Marjorie was working on a canvas, really a semiabstract still life of a very prosaic table with flowers and fruit. She found herself blocked. She couldn't go on. She stared at the canvas for some time. Then, as though she'd had an inspiration, she began to make broad circular movements with the brush over the large canvas that stood on her easel. She had paint on the brush but didn't touch the canvas. She shifted around or near the canvas in odd eurythmic movements until suddenly she reached out and swiftly daubed some color on the charcoal outlines of the still life before her. It was just a small, slashing cut that squirmed its way down for about six inches.

I was in the studio watching her as I often did, coming in from time to time when I needed a breather from the novel I happened to be working on. I said nothing, just watched.

Again the eurythmic movements for several seconds, then another dart at the canvas, this time with a different brush and new colors mixed straight off her palette, which consisted of a square of glass set on top of a low table alongside the easel. This series of movements that seemed to resemble a ritual dance followed by action on the canvas went on for almost an hour. By then the scattered daubs were beginning to take shape, as though she had been connecting a series of dots to form a hidden figure. And as that first figure began to emerge, I was the one to recognize it. There was nothing abstract about it. In fact, the precisely painted forms fell together into a shape I recognized as the figure of Ganesa, the Hindu god of power and wealth, whose elephant form is widely known all over India.

I was familiar with the Hindu pantheon through my poking around in comparative religion and Eastern iconography, but Marjorie knew nothing about it. All of her schooling had been Western. Nevertheless, as she continued, more and more of these figures began to appear until a crowd of them filled the canvas, replete with such fine details that they might have been copied out of a book except for the unusual pastel softness of the color so that each figure seemed to be emerging from some matrix of pure light. There were representations of Shiva, the radiant visage of Gautama Buddha, Mara, the god of death, and numerous others I recognized without recalling precisely which was who.

Marjorie was confounded. She found it almost impossible to believe she had painted all these things. Where did they come from? What hidden aspect of self had she stumbled on? Why now? What unrecognized inner prompting had enabled her to evoke this buried store of visual treasure? Then she recalled what Jackson had said: "I just do it."

"And that's what I suppose I did," she tried to explain, both to me and to herself. "I just did it. But—I don't like it. I mean, I don't know where it's coming from." She waved her arms at it in exasperation. "Take it away! That's not how I want to paint. There's nothing of mine in it."

"Maybe," I suggested, "it takes a combination of both. Of your input and the input from unknown sources. Maybe that's what inspiration is."

"Anyway," Marjorie said, treating the whole matter with a kind of nervous disdain, "we have some shopping to do. I'll let this go now. I'd better write out a grocery list."

She picked up a pencil and started jotting items down on the back of an old envelope. For a moment everything seemed normal again. And then it wasn't normal at all.

The pencil unaccountably jumped in her hand, crossing out two of the items listed. And then it proceeded to write, "Fish and fowl. You are no longer meat-eaters."

I knew it was the pencil and not Marjorie. She was as startled as I was.

We looked at each other. Clearly it wasn't all going to lend itself to a neat if complicated explanation like gravitational fields formed by charged circles on a canvas. There wasn't any gravitational field here. There was a presence we didn't know. The force surely came from Marjorie, but it was one she didn't recognize and wasn't ready to acknowledge.

"I'm getting a message," she said suddenly, turning pale. "It says I'm to take a bath and sit quietly for a while before the canvas and then paint. But I'm not supposed to tell you anything about it."

"Oh no—a voice?"

"No voice. I just know what it's telling me."

"What do you make of it?"

"I'm not supposed to make anything of it. Some part of me is dipping into some other part I never knew about. That's all I can say."

Marjorie obeyed the injunction to bathe. Then she sat in front of the canvas for a while. And suddenly she started working again, starting something entirely new, right over the Hindu images she had only recently created. I watched her nervously.

"I feel I shouldn't tell you this, but it's not something that belongs to me—this force," she said. "It's more as if I belong to it—"

And scarcely had she uttered these words than her face contorted;

she dropped her brush and bent way over, her hands clutching at her chest. "I—I can't breathe—"

I had seen reactions like that before when a friend was having a sudden heart attack. I grabbed her and told her to hold on. Frightened, gasping and struggling for breath, she clung to me as I managed to get her to the car. She sat beside me, pale, agitated, taking harsh, short breaths as I drove like a maniac to the office of the local doctor.

"It's like a—a short circuit," she managed to explain. "I feel as though the—" She broke off and took a couple of quick breaths. "As though everything in me is disrupted. It—it isn't flowing—smoothly. I never—noticed—before. It happened—because I wasn't supposed to tell you—as though I broke some kind of—of—"

"Circuit?" I said.

She nodded. "I can feel all this kind of—wild power—chasing around—inside—"

"Don't talk. It's all right. I've heard of things like this happening when people try to do yoga without a proper teacher. They force the power up through the vital centers—the chakras—before they're ready. Maybe—"

But we were already at the doctor's office which was nearby. We went in. The receptionist looked at us in alarm. She said we'd have to wait just the same. The doctor was busy on another emergency at the moment. Should she call an ambulance, or could we hold on?

We decided to wait. We sat down in adjacent chairs while the receptionist went off somewhere, probably to warn the doctor.

I'm not one who can claim any kind of second sight. If I get inspirations, they're usually because there's been a lot of sweat and fomenting of stuff first. But this time I really had a wild idea, and I knew it was going to work. To this day, I haven't the least idea why. But I held my hands out toward Marjorie, my right wrist crossed over my left. "Do what I'm doing," I told her. "Cross your hands at the wrist and grab my fingers."

By now passive with fear, she didn't question me. She reached out and clung tightly to my outstretched hands. As she did I felt a swift surge of force rushing up my arms and through my body. It wasn't nearly as severe as what she must have experienced. It was even strangely exhilarating, as though I'd just swallowed some speed. The tension seemed to fade from her fingertips. I saw her body loosen as she began taking deeper, easier breaths.

"It's better," she said. "I can feel it flowing out of me. What did you do?"

"You're all right now?"

"I think so. It all just—smoothed out. How did you—"

"I don't know," I said. I looked around the waiting room. The receptionist still hadn't returned. A new thought struck me.

"You're sure you're all right?"

She took another deep breath and nodded. "It's all gone now."

"I was just thinking—"

"What?"

"When the doctor comes out—what'll we tell him?" I suddenly had visions of him sending for little men in white coats once he heard our story. Marjorie nodded. She was thinking the same thing.

"Let's get out of here," I said.

Marjorie nodded again. We got up. We didn't just leave. We fled.

These long shards of memory kept stabbing at me as I sat at that Chock Full o' Nuts counter. And what had they to do with whether or not I should agree to write Superman? Precisely this: that there really had to be some sort of deeper hidden self of which our outward Clark Kent personality was but the dim reflection. I didn't understand all of it yet. But it was clear enough to me that if I tried to write Superman, if they let me do the stories my own way, if they let me explore more fully that division between the ordinary and the extraordinary so clearly manifested in "the Man of Steel," it would mean something more than just doing another comic strip with superpowered monsters punching each other out. On that basis, then, I made up my mind, went back upstairs to the office, and told my editor I was ready to take on Superman.

In the end I did mostly just Batman and Superman, with an understandable predilection for Superman, which included series titles like Superboy and Lois Lane and Jimmy Olsen. But my greatest freedom in exploring the character came when I wrote the daily newspaper strip. In that genre especially I had free rein to explore every aspect of the elements I found interesting in the character. You might even say that in order to write the "daily" my way, I had to create my own Superman.

I worked in comics for nineteen years. During that time I probably produced the equivalent of twenty thousand comics pages. And I maintained what I can only call a special relationship with Superman, although I had no idea in those days how deep that relationship went. Of course I was bound to find Superman an interesting subject as I came more and more to visualize him in his mythic proportions. How I gradually changed the character, revealing some of his hitherto unexplored aspects, is another story and wouldn't have been possible except for the support and sensitivity of Jack Schiff, my editor.

Sometime in 1958, however, an editor named Mort Weisinger took over the Superman books from Jack Schiff. This was something of a problem because I much preferred working with Schiff. Like most others, I found Weisinger difficult to deal with. But I endured until one day he insisted that I write a story in which Superman finds some way to transfer his powers to Lois Lane. I didn't want to do that story. I thought such a plot was out of character. In a deeper sense I thought a certain quintessential element of Superman's reality, as I understood it, would be compromised if he could transfer his powers so capriciously. So I wrote the story under protest. And then I left. The charm was broken. I never wrote comics again.

Before meeting Thongden I had never bothered to ask myself why I made such a big issue of that strip. After all, I was also a regular writer on Batman, and often enough I had written Batman stories that I thought might have been uncharacteristic. But working on Batman was one thing. My relationship with Superman was quite another. Still, it took decades before I understood that relationship clearly enough to set it down here. When I left comics, I thought I was through with Superman. I was far from through, but I didn't know that before Thongden showed up in my life. As I sat in my kitchen in utter confusion after that first visit from a monk who claimed to be a *tulpa*, Superman's lingering influence on my life was just on the verge of revealing itself to me.

Thongden's improbable visit had the immediate effect of bringing back those earlier extraordinary events. Mostly for reassurance, I needed to remind myself that strange things do happen from time to time. But it also struck me at that moment how I had defensively buried those earlier experiences among the rubble at the back of my mind. And that realization triggered still another memory, one that linked all of it together in one meaningful chain.

In the summer of 1965, I had gone on a vacation to Hawaii. During my stay there an older member of the staff of the old Bishop Museum in Honolulu told me about a man named J. A. K. Coombs who had witnessed one of the island's *kahunas* accomplish a truly miraculous healing. I had read about Hawaii's *kahunas* before and knew that they were a kind of shaman to whom all sorts of supernormal abilities were attributed.

Coombs was related by marriage, though somewhat distantly, to an old woman reputed to be one of the most powerful *kahunas* in the islands. In fact, Coombs witnessed the extraordinary event firsthand at a party at the woman's home. Apparently one of the guests took a bad fall from the overhanging deck of the house to the beach, severely damaging his leg. The fracture was so complete that the broken bones thrust out against the skin. Coombs immediately decided that the man had to be rushed to the hospital. But the old woman whom he described as his "grandmother-in-law" put her foot down. She would take care of the injured man, she announced. And she proceeded to do so by praying and performing certain incantations. At no point did she actually touch the man, but after some moments she rose and announced that his leg was healed. The man, puzzled, got gingerly to his feet, tried to take some steps, discovered that he could safely navigate, and finally began walking about as though nothing had happened.[1]

Now, I had heard many a story over the years about miraculous healings and unusual cures, so this would have been one more story that might also have remained filed away in the back of my mind except for a subsequent trip to Hawaii three years later. That was when I met Harry.

I was sitting on the beach in front of my hotel when this squat little man of clearly Polynesian ancestry, about sixty years old, wearing one of those gaudy printed Hawaiian shirts, a pair of shorts, and an old peaked cap, sat down alongside me. I recognized him then as one of the hotel employees, someone who did various odd jobs from baggage hauling to cleaning to room service—a man cheerful, energetic, and constantly smiling when he wasn't tucked away in some corner quietly reading a comic book.

"My name is Harry," he announced.

"Alvin," I responded, wondering why he had sought me out.

"Glad to know you, Al," he said familiarly.

There was a moment of silence. Then Harry remarked, "We have something in common."

"We do? What might that be, Harry?"

He shrugged. "I don't know. But I feel it." Then, noticing my puzzlement, he added as though it explained everything, "I am a *kahuna*."

"You mean your inner sight told you?"

"Yeah—something like that. What business you in, Al?"

"I'm a writer," I said.

"That's a good thing," Harry said cryptically. "What you write?"

"Probably nothing you'd know about right now. But—I used to write Superman."

"I think that's it," Harry said. "I used to know Superman."

"You used to *know* Superman? You mean—you read Superman comics?"

Harry shook his head. "No—I mean I knew Superman personally."

"Of course," I said in quiet dismissal.

"You think I'm pulling your leg?"

"You can put it that way."

Harry chuckled. "I'll tell you something, Al. You wouldn't be sitting here on this beach right now if it hadn't been for me and Superman."

"I'll bet," I said once more.

But Harry didn't dismiss so easily. He shook his head. "You're a writer. You should be looser than that." He reflected for a moment. "I'll explain something to you," he said finally. "You got a theory of what's real and what's not real."

"I suppose I do," I admitted. "Like everyone else."

"You think it's reliable?"

"What do you mean?"

"Well, you know, a theory is supposed to be a way of looking at the world. There's no guarantee it's true. Truth is too big for us. Think about that."

"I see I'm in the hands of a philosopher."

"Only in your own hands, Al." He dipped his stick into the sand and doodled with it for a moment. "So—all I was saying is a theory doesn't tell us nothing about what's out there. It only gives us some operating principles, you know, to deal with certain problems. Nobody knows the whole story."

"Well—"

"Let's say like you approach somebody and you got a fixed theory about him. Like you look at me and decide I'm a little crazy. So everything I say after that, you'll explain by my craziness. You see, your theory proves itself. It feeds you back what you believe. Like when Newton discovered gravity, everybody saw things as explained by gravity. But how come for thousands of years before that people got along fine without gravity? You get it? What you believe is what gets fed back to you. But there's a lot your theories don't take into account. Like me meeting Superman."

"But—" I was trying to protest. And then something about the way he looked at me led me to say, "Tell me about Superman."

Harry continued doodling in the sand. "You know," he said, "geologists are just now finding out that a long time back these islands were almost destroyed by a big undersea volcano."

"I read about that somewhere," I acknowledged, glad we could find some common ground.

"They would have been destroyed too—except for Superman."

"But that eruption occurred eons ago," I protested, "when there was no Superman."

"That's where your theory of reality trips you up," Harry said. "Time isn't really something that passes, Al. That's just your way of thinking. Didn't you ever ask yourself how come time can pass if it wasn't all there at once?" Harry shook his head. "But there's no use my telling you about time. You think it's a one-way street."

"So how did you and Superman save these islands two thousand years ago?" I asked, trying to keep Harry on track.

"Well, I was the one that asked him to do it."

"Two thousand years ago?"

"No—I asked him—well, I guess it was—" Harry began counting on his fingers. "Maybe five years ago," he said. "And don't look at me like that with your theory that I'm crazy. Just listen."

"Okay," I said, feeling curious and foolish at the same time.

"I had gone to visit my great-great—many times great—grandfather. Not here on Oahu. We met on Hawaii, the biggest island. Two thousand years back from where we are."

Suddenly I felt a mean little glow of triumph. Now, I thought, I had him. "Harry—your great-great-ancestor wasn't even living here two thousand years ago. There were no Polynesian settlements that far back."

"That's right," Harry said, unperturbed. "But my ancestors had come to these islands many times before they actually settled here. They thought the islands were too unstable. But anyway, my ancestor—Grandpa—he summoned me, and we had this meeting on Hawaii. And he said this was going to be a good place for a lot of our families to settle—"

"You met him here two thousand years ago?"

"In my *kahuna* body, of course. That's what we do, you know? We visit with our ancestors all the time. That's what keeps things together."

"I see."

"But Grandpa was worried that the volcano would blow up the islands, and no one among us had the power to stop it. That's when I told him Superman could stop it. And I said I'd try to get in touch with him."

I shook my head. This was getting wilder and wilder. "And how would you manage to do that?"

Harry shrugged. "Write a letter care of the *Daily Planet*."

"But there is no—"

Harry laid his stick down in the sand and tapped me on the arm. He was smiling. "That's one of the things a *kahuna* knows how to do," he assured me. "Anyway, we met on the beach," Harry said. "Right near this very spot. It was a day of big rain. Nobody else was around."

"Of course," I said, making no effort to conceal my skepticism.

"I told him the problem, and he told me he couldn't do it. That was when I said to him, 'Of course you can do it. In fact, you already did it. Otherwise we wouldn't be sitting here on this beach right now.' That stymied him. He looked at me and shook his head. 'I'm not sure I can argue with a man who can time-travel.'

31

"'At least,' I told him, 'you've got an open mind,'" Harry narrated. "'Now in that movie where you flew so fast you time-traveled back a few minutes so you could save Lois Lane's life—do you remember that?' And he grinned at me and said, 'I'm afraid I never saw that movie.' He held his hands out. 'I don't have much time for that sort of thing.' 'Anyway,' I said, 'The question is, are you ready to try going back in time?' And he said, 'I don't know. But if I don't, will we all just disappear from this beach because Hawaii doesn't exist?' And then I told him that he'd have to take my word as a *kahuna* that it wouldn't be good if we all just disappeared. And besides, I didn't have the answer. The main thing was—would he try it? Well—he thought a while and then said with a funny look on his face, 'Since I already did it, I guess I may as well go ahead. It wouldn't seem right not to have Hawaii around anyway.'"

"That's quite a story," I said to Harry.

"Well," Harry said, "Superman went ahead and fixed things." He shrugged. "He always does, doesn't he?"

"Does he?" I said, feeling a bit defensive for some reason.

"Let me explain something to you about volcanoes," Harry said. "Because when you look at the islands today, the volcanoes are gentle, well behaved. They call them shield volcanoes. The magma is very fluid and erupts quietly—very ladylike, I would say. They even look a little like shields. But they weren't always that way, Al. When Superman came, the magmas had a lot of deadly gas, and they were thick and very explosive. They would blow high into the sky, and then the magma would come pouring down like bombs. Some of it's just ash, but some of it's as big as a house. Nothing you want to be around when it's happening. That's why Grandpa wanted something done about it. Because otherwise these islands wouldn't be such a paradise, as you can see for yourself, Al."

He paused, looking at me expectantly as though hoping I'd comment.

"And that's why we're here today," I concluded for him.

"Let me tell you," Harry said, "it wasn't an easy job—not even for Superman."

"If you say so."

"You should be more open to things," Harry added, sounding a little disapproving. And then this little man in the funny cap and the flashy shirt who did odd jobs around the hotel had some parting words for me. He stood up, ready to leave, but first he touched his hand to my forehead.

"One day," he said, "you'll find out for yourself what thinking can do. The power of thought is sometimes more than the thinker. Lucky most people don't understand that. They think so many different thoughts that nothing much happens, which is probably a good thing. But lately a lot of angels are being created. That's right. Angels. Where do you think all the books and stories about angels come from? Out of thin air? No. Because people need help and don't know where to turn, so they look for guardian angels, and the power gets formed, and the angels are there, And sometimes they can help. Up to a point. Then there are the people who create space aliens, But mostly they're very confused about what they want from aliens, you know? Anyway, you—you'll learn."

Oddly enough, I already had, I remembered as I sat on that beach toward the end of the '60s. And I had forgotten. I had forgotten about that night at Jackson Pollock's studio. I had forgotten about that irruption of Hindu images from Marjorie's entranced brush. I had almost forgotten Marjorie. We had long since gone our separate ways, and I had remarried soon after. That second marriage proved to be the most enduring thing in my life, in more ways than one. As I thought of Harry's story, I recalled an old Hasidic tale related by the Hebrew philosopher Martin Buber about a rabbi who used to get up very early in the morning and wash the dishes even though he had washed them only the evening before. One day when a pupil asked the rabbi why he got up so early to wash the dishes again, the rabbi replied, "Because the dust gathers on the dishes every night."

I told myself as Harry started to stride away up the beach that when strange and wondrous things happen, and they do happen to each of us, we suppose that we'll never forget them. But we do indeed forget. Because the dust gathers every night. If we wish to hold on to those wondrous experiences, we have to make an effort to do so. We need to find ways of reminding ourselves. So before Harry could get out of earshot, I called out to him as though he knew *when* I would receive that new and fresh reminder.

"When will that be?" I said.

Harry shrugged. "Whenever," he said cryptically. And then he turned, and I watched him walk back up the beach toward the hotel.

Chapter Three

Suddenly, as I sat in my kitchen almost three decades after Hawaii and a half hour after Thongden's departure, I knew that Harry's "whenever" had just happened. For a while I remained frozen in my chair, filled with the certainty that *this was it*. This time I knew I was not going to let myself prejudge anything. Whatever it was that this mysterious Mr. Thongden meant or stood for, I would not dismiss him with some easy notion of what I expected reality to be. I wasn't going to let the dust gather on the dishes again.

Kay, my wife for the past forty years, is what her friends like to call an "earthy" person. She even takes my fantasizing, of which I do a lot, in her own earthy, accepting way. "That's what Alvin is like. Maybe it's important to be that way to write the kind of books he does." She's also earthy in a physical way. She's unusually strong for a small woman just past sixty. She can do heavy work like pushing furniture around and lifting boxes, not to mention spending hours in her garden digging and spading and weeding, work that would tire a deskbound creature like me in minutes, though I'm still in reasonably good shape, considering. She got back from the mall, and because the whole episode with Thongden had left such a powerful impression on me, I had to tell her all about it right away.

I should have realized how she'd react. She laughed. She was standing at the kitchen sink opening a large package of chicken breasts, which she was separating into two parts, one for the dinner she planned for that night, the other to be put away in the freezer. "Is this your great new idea?"

"What idea?"

"For your new book. The one you're trying to start. What else?"

"No—no—it's not an idea. He was really here. I know you find it hard to accept such things, but—it happened."

"If you say so."

"I'm telling you, it really did. It happened. I had a—a visitation."

She was sealing the second package for the freezer. "Well, you always did like to believe in your characters," she acknowledged. "But you don't have to push it so far with me. I'm glad you've got an idea, anyway. It's not easy having you stomping around here trying to get started on a new book. Let's hope this one works out."

I went up to her, took her by the shoulders, and turned her around to face me. "Kay—he really was here. He sat in that chair. He drank out of that cup." I pointed to the tabletop before I noticed that the cup was gone. Perhaps Kay had already put it into the dishwasher.

She gave me a troubled look. "A man was really here?" she said. "You're not just trying something out on me?"

"Can't you tell I'm not making it up?"

She sat down at the table and studied me. "So someone came here and gave you this crazy story. And you believed him. I mean—what else do you expect me to say? I know how gullible you are."

"Why would anyone want to do that?"

"With some of your crazy friends, does there have to be a reason?"

I took the adjacent seat and looked out the window again. "I suppose it's possible," I admitted. But deep within me, I was certain. I knew Thongden was real.

* * *

We didn't discuss it any further that afternoon and evening, but I sat and thought about it. And I realized that that was exactly what Thongden wanted me to do. It made a kind of sense, especially to an old science fiction buff like me. How many times had I read about silicon life forms that survived by draining electric current from the city power grid? Or creatures that needed to frighten people because their metabolism depended on strong emotions? So why not a life form created by thought and needing fresh thought to survive? I even remembered that in one of his Mars stories, Edgar Rice Burroughs had conjured up legions of deadly bowmen who were themselves nothing but the thought creations of the being who manipulated them. But—I wasn't a science fiction writer. And I wasn't a character in a science fiction story, either, Kay took the trouble of reminding me of this fact at breakfast the next morning. I didn't protest. After sleeping on the event, I let myself appear to believe that Thongden wasn't quite as real as he had seemed at first. Since I couldn't think of any easy way to convert Kay to my own unique certainty, I knew this path would be a smoother one to follow. But I had figured out how I might put it all to an objective test.

A few days later I had a luncheon date with my agent in New York. She wouldn't tell me what it was about over the phone when she called. "Just something I need to go over with you," she insisted, "eyeball to eyeball."

"Can you tell me at least whether its something good or something bad?"

"We'll both know after I see you," she said.

I drove to Harmon Station, parked the car, and took the train to Grand Central.

"I know you're working hard at trying to get started on a new book," she told me. "I wanted to get at you before the process carried you too far out of my reach." Hedy Greene was wearing what I used to call her landed-gentry outfit. It was something I'd noticed she wore only when she needed to signal the occasion was special. I don't know how she dressed when she saw publishers or any of her best-selling authors. For me, most of the time, she wore outfits so ordinary that I didn't notice them enough to be able to describe them. But today was different. Today she wore her frowsy reddish-brown tweed jacket and skirt with the kind of old-fashioned English tailoring designed to last forever in total disdain of the foibles of fashion. It must have been at least ten years old because I remember her wearing it on the day she gave me my first check for the first novel she sold for me. Two years later she took me to lunch at Hammond's, a small basement place on East 53rd that was mostly frequented by literary types. On that occasion she very earnestly advised me that even though I was well past the first flush of youth, I should try to give my late-blooming talent its full rein and not write for the marketplace. "You'll make less money, of course, but you'll have a more solid feeling about yourself. That's really what counts in the end, don't you think?" It had been an important meeting because I'd been struggling over that problem with myself, and somehow Hedy intervened to help me to my decision at just the right time. The result was that I was really beginning to enjoy what I was doing and, at the same time, beginning to earn moderate critical success. The money wasn't great, but it was enough, and Hedy got her own personal satisfaction out of the way I was going. She was a decade younger than I, yet she had a way of mothering me that I really appreciated.

So here we were, at Hammond's again and clearly onstage at another momentous occasion. There were other signs besides the landed-gentry outfit, but they were subtler. I felt them in the way she surveyed me as though wondering how far she might intrude on me. She was preparing to do her mothering but needed my connivance. I reached across the table and took her hand.

"Hedy—if I need telling off, I'm ready to listen. Only I thought my last manuscript—it is about the last one, isn't it?" I was referring to the longish book I had delivered to her more than two weeks earlier. "I thought it was just what the muses ordered. Wasn't it? You didn't like it."

"It was all right," she said without much enthusiasm.

"Uh-oh. Maybe you'd better just give it to me straight."

"I can probably sell it," she said. "But for your sake, I'm not sure I should."

"That bad?" I said, feeling a dry, tight pull in my epigastric region.

"No—it wasn't bad. It's just that you're slowly writing your way out of the new zeitgeist, and I don't think I should encourage you."

"Look—it's not my fault if publishers don't turn handsprings over literary writers. I thought you said I should ignore all that and—"

"That's not it," she interrupted. "It's not a question of publishers' venality, of accountants running the business—all that stuff I hear a thousand times a week. Not in your case, anyway. You didn't do what we agreed you had to do. You're still trying to follow a safe, conventional model. Full of these tantalizing hints of a unique vision. But in the end you always back away. And what we get is neither fish nor fowl. Midlist at best. Alvin, you've got to let it loose. Give us all of it."

I was silent for a while—too shocked to say anything.

"I'm sorry," she said. "But maybe I have to bully the next book out of you. It's what makes this all worthwhile for me too."

I smiled at her. Maybe it was more of a grimace than a smile. "I've got this idea," I began. "Coming down this morning, I thought maybe it was too wild—it has to do with—well—something about the ability of the imagination to create reality."

She didn't even blink. "I thought that was always the point," she said.

"I mean—literally."

"Of course literally. Literally, we create our own reality. The world is the way we see it." I didn't realize that she truly meant something about the flexibility of reality that I hadn't yet begun to grasp. It was still another signal to me—a kind of synchronicity, connected to Thongden but in a noncausal way. But I wasn't hearing her properly. Instead I followed my own train of thought.

"Listen—a few days ago this character comes to see me. Literally. And it turns out he isn't real. I mean, not real the way you and I are real. But otherwise he's just like us. You can touch him and talk to him. The only difference is, he was never born. He was conjured out of someone's imagination." I'd hardly said it when I backed away. "Just a premise, of course."

"Leading to what?" was all she said.

"It's something I'm just starting to explore."

"I hope you're not trying to write comics again—in book form. Those new graphic novels—"

"Hedy, that's not fair, I got your message. If you hadn't said what you did, maybe I wouldn't have mentioned this particular springboard. But I'm going to follow it through. Whether or not you or anyone else approves of it."

She looked at me. Then she shrugged and presented me with one of her hieratic smiles. "I suppose I asked for it," she confessed. "All right. Let's see. In the meantime, what do you want me to do with your last manuscript?"

"What do *you* think?"

"I think I should hold it for a while until you can show me some chapters of your new project. Then we'll see. Does that suit you? Can you afford not to sell this one right off?"

I suddenly felt very sure of myself. "As you said, I really can't afford to sell it either," I said. "So why don't we wait a while?"

As soon as Hedy and I parted, I went into the first phone booth I could find and got hold of a Manhattan directory. There was a listing for a D. Thongden on West 89th Street. There was no other Thongden in the book. I wrote down the number and the address, but I had no intention of phoning. Thongden had established a precedent by dropping in on me, and I intended to return the favor. I wanted to see him in his own place, amid his own things, conducting his own life, whatever that might be.

I walked west and took a Broadway bus north to 88th Street, walked the extra block to 89th Street, and turned right toward Riverside Drive on a street fronted on both sides by identical two-story old brownstones, at least half of which had been partitioned from single-family dwellings into as many as three and four separate apartments. Each building had the same flight of brownstone steps and heavy brownstone balustrades leading to the double front doors. In a number of the houses, heavy metal doors had been substituted for the original glass-paneled ones or the glass itself had been either boarded over or covered with an ironwork grill. These architectural mutations were relatively recent, having been acquired gradually during the past decade in response to the city's rising climate of violence. But Thongden's building, about halfway down and on the south side of the street, seemed not to have adopted any of these changes. Even the original glass doors were still in place.

Seated side by side halfway up the front steps were two men, both squat and burly looking, who might have been a pair of Japanese sumo wrestlers in identical brown suits. Or could they have been Tibetan? To my untutored eye, this was highly possible, and Thongden might well have chosen to live among compatriots.

Normally these side streets off upper Broadway were fairly active places, with people on the steps at all hours and kids playing in the street and voices raised in a babel of Spanish and English. But not today. It was simply too cold to be sitting outside. With the exception of the unprepossessing pair blocking the steps at Thongden's place, no one on that whole street was outside. It struck me as I approached that if these two were known residents of that building, it surely would have no need of barricaded doors or iron grills. I began to feel some trepidation about presenting myself unannounced and wondered whether this unlikely pair of hippogriffs would let me pass.

Despite the tightness in my stomach, I strode boldly toward the building, mounted the first few steps, and waited for the pair to move aside. They didn't. They didn't utter a word either but simply looked at me with dark, expressionless eyes.

"I'm here to see Mr. Thongden," I announced. "He does live here, doesn't he?"

"Oh," said the one on the left in the mildest of voices. "Mr. Thongden." The Oriental flattening of the *r* sound was very much in evidence, along with shortening of the other phonemes of the name as I uttered it. "You are Mr. Schwartz?" As he spoke, they both rose and stepped aside, each to the opposite balustrade, making room for me to pass.

"He was expecting me?" I said, surprised, but only modestly, as though I were already conditioned to the unlikely where Thongden was concerned.

"No—but he think maybe you come."

"Of course," I said. And for lack of anything else to say, I added, "And—you're his neighbors?"

My question elicited an exchange of smiles between the pair. The first one, still smiling, turned to me with a slight bow. "Sometimes," he said.

"And which is Mr. Thongden's apartment?"

"All same," the man replied. Adding, in response to my puzzled look, "Only one apartment."

"Thanks," I murmured and walked on past to the door, where I looked in vain for the usual brass doorbell.

"Door open," my adviser said. "Just go in."

I tried the door, and it opened easily. I stepped into a hallway dimly lit by the daylight filtering through the glass door. After some moments I could make out double French doors just ahead and to the left. There was a glow coming through them, enough to reveal to my adjusting vision the lineaments of the far end of the hallway. I ventured slowly toward the French doors and peered in. To my surprise, there was only a gray-blue opacity. I couldn't see into the room, though the glass was clear enough. Whatever was blocking my vision was coming from inside. I stood for a moment, hesitant. Then I tried a tentative rap on one of the door panes. I waited perhaps twenty seconds, but there was no response. Impatient, I pushed the door open and found myself staring at—nothing. Not exactly nothing, just more of the same opaque gray-blue expanse. It appeared to be a billowing monochrome curtain of some kind with an inestimable gauzy depth. I stepped into the room and reached out to touch the grayness, but there was nothing there.

Over the silence I heard the faint sound of running water accompanied by a ratcheting noise, as though someone were operating an old hand pump. I had acquired some knowledge of these in various country places I'd lived in, and the sound was unmistakable. Then, as I stood there wondering, the gauzy obstruction seemed to thin out at the center, opening slowly as though revealing a portion of a stage set, and I found myself staring at a long wooden sink on which piles of heavy dishes were stacked. As the grayness continued to roll back, I saw a small, thin man bending over one end of the long tub. As he wielded the pump handle from which water spurted, he took dishes down from the stack, one or two at a time, and let the fresh runnels splash over them. The little man was wearing a *yarmulke* and his small frame was covered with a large white shawl edged with fringe and decorated in light blue—a *tallith*. And he was softly humming a tantalizingly familiar melody in some bright pentatonic scale. I didn't have to be told who he was. As he worked he kept tapping his foot to the rhythm of his own song, almost as though he were dancing. I knew him as well as I knew my own mind. He was the rabbi I had so often forgotten to emulate, the one who got up early in the morning and washed the dishes!

Clearly this whole thing had been set up for my benefit. But even assuming that Thongden really was the *tulpa* he claimed to be—how could he have known? Again I experienced that eeriness I'd first felt when Thongden had turned up at my home and managed at least partially to convince me of what he was. Clearly this scene dredged from my own memories was supposed to remind me that I'd let the dust gather too long on—what? Maybe something to do with that image of Superman he'd mentioned at our first meeting. As this notion occurred to me, I heard my name.

"Mr. Schwartz!"

The sharp, clear sound came from the far right. It was a woman's voice in whose melting tones my name seemed to go through a gentle rise in frequency like a reversed echo. I turned to see her step out of the shadows to stand directly under a large, lighted candelabrum that flickered over the scene from a high shelf at the far end of the sink, as though to complete the medieval imagery. She had a long, narrow face, dark hair, and eyes that were large and gray and far apart. She wore a trailing green gown that clung to her tall, full frame as it tumbled enticingly down to her ankles. And she was so beautiful, I knew she couldn't possibly be real.

"Yes?" I said in a rasping whisper of sheer confusion.

She turned and went through a door at the room's far end that I hadn't seen until, as she opened it, a flash of brightness glinted across the threshold. I followed her into this other room just in time to see her disappearing behind a curtained alcove at the farther end. There, his long body folded into a high-backed fan chair directly in front of me, dressed in a light gray flannel suit that only a skilled and expensive tailor could have fitted to that ungainly frame, was Mr. Thongden. He sat with one leg crossed over the other, his hands resting daintily on his lap. His hair was neatly blow-dried in place, and he looked for all the world like a wealthy and successful Eurasian businessman.

"Good to see you," Thongden said. "Please sit down. But don't look so astonished. What you see is what there is, as I'm sure you'll come to understand in due course."

Chapter Four

Thongden began his explanation by asking me to open the door I had just passed through and peer back into that other room. I did so.

Every sign of the rabbi and his dishes and his sink had vanished.

There were now only a plain table and four chairs, along with the heavy matching sideboard that stood in the place of the sink crammed only moments before by the stacks of unwashed dishes. Thongden had exercised some sort of pointed illusion for my benefit.

"Very impressive," I said, turning back to him. "You're a regular Houdini. I guess now I'm supposed to ask how you did it?"

"A kind of mental hologram," he declared, adding, "with your help, of course."

"Of course," I said. "Obviously I was the audience."

"No—no," he said. He urged me to sit down, put aside my preconceptions, and hear him out. I settled down somewhat stiffly in the chair facing him.

"I'm all ears," I said.

This brought a broad grin to Thongden's flat, saturnine features, "I like that expression. Very vivid. I never heard it before. Is it common?"

"I'm all ears?" I repeated. "It's common enough." He couldn't avoid noticing that I fairly bristled with annoyance at his little games, and this was apparently his way of trying to soften my mood. "Yes—very common," I repeated.

He waggled his head, the smile still ruffling his naturally stiff mien. "I had this image of you almost completely covered with large ears—a literal listening post."

"Well—" I responded vaguely, unable to stifle a grin of my own.

"To get on, then," Thongden resumed. "I prepared a demonstration especially for you. I produced the dishwashing scene in that room just so you could see how your thinking about me has restored my capacity for image materialization. Both a demonstration and an expression of gratitude. Naturally I'm aware that you couldn't have avoided thinking about me. Not the way I suddenly presented myself to you at your home yesterday. But it is my hope that you and I will continue to work together in a special symbiosis for the foreseeable future."

"Now, wait a minute," I started to protest.

"You must hear me out," he urged. "There is much to explain."

"All right—but the man in that room—the rabbi—those materializations, as you called them. You couldn't have done it without reading my mind."

"Ah—yes—inspired by yourself. I didn't choose the rabbi. You did. I had no idea what would appear. The rabbi, in fact, to use a word you mistakenly applied to me yesterday, was an apparition. A shadow—a musical shadow, if you like. A distortion of the light. Or better still, a hologram. A set of interference patterns in which you participated. But not at all like you and me."

I couldn't help noticing how he'd put himself on the same level of reality as I, and it disturbed me to consider myself no more real than a *tulpa*. If he *was* a *tulpa*.

"It takes a long time to create a *tulpa*," he went on as though reading my thoughts. "Nine months at the very least. Just like an ordinary viviparous birth. You see, we are both real in the same way, apart from differences in the processes that created us. On the other hand, we have different metabolic needs and capacities. You must ingest fruits of the earth to maintain full functioning. You eat. You have a digestive system and a veritable internal electrochemical factory that transforms and distributes the energy required for your functioning. While I—I require . . . mind energy. I think that's the best term for it. If there's no one to think about me—I lose substance. I fade away. You see?"

I shook my head. "There's something wrong about all this," I insisted. "It's too far-fetched. There's a gimmick somewhere. But even assuming for the moment that it's exactly as you say—how did you manage until now without my help? And why do you come to me now?"

"To answer the last question first—it was that Superman article you wrote. As I tried to explain, you had a bias toward the notion that life can be materialized out of thought. You were, I might say, halfway there. Finding myself where I am, in a culture that's totally antithetical to such notions, it seemed to me you were easily my best hope. It may take some additional convincing, but at least you offer me something to work with."

"But what are you doing in this apparently hostile culture? And how did you manage to survive until now?"

Thongden fixed his strange amber eyes upon me for some moments without saying anything. Finally he asked, "Did you ever hear of Everett Nelson?"

The name sounded familiar, but I couldn't quite place it. "Some kind of linguistic scholar?" I guessed, reaching down through some faint threads of memory.

"In a way, yes. He was a student of W. Y. Evans-Wentz, the scholar who first translated the *Tibetan Book of the Dead* into English.

Nelson followed in his footsteps and shared many of his interests. Like Evans-Wentz, he was more than just a skilled linguist. He was a true *rimpoche*."

I sat stiffly on the edge of my chair, watching him. "I have no idea what that word means."

"Sorry. I knew of course that you didn't. But it just came naturally to me. Means something like—well, in English, of course, you'd say lama. Kind of a priest. Only a little more than that."

I nodded. "How could you know what I know or don't know? You did say you 'knew' I didn't know?"

He looked at me now as though weighing whether he should answer. It wasn't so much reluctance I read on his features as a certain delicacy, a concern for my feelings. Finally he came to a decision. "Instead of answering that directly, let's step back a few paces, as you might say. I brought up Dr. Nelson's name because he was the man who created me. In other words, he thought me up."

I was about to protest, not about that particular statement but generally, about the whole conversation. It was too much to take in all at once. I started to get out of my chair in the process.

"No—don't. Hear me out. This part is important."

"What part?"

Thongden gave an audible sigh and lowered his head as he spoke softly, avoiding my eyes as though what he was revealing now were somehow too private to put to me directly. "I lost Dr. Nelson about a week ago."

Suddenly I remembered where I had heard the name. I'd read it in the paper. Nelson had died in his Oxford home, apparently of old age, and was an important enough scholar to merit a two-column obituary recounting, among other things, his great work in translating important Tibetan texts. The article had also mentioned that Everett Nelson was considered something of a sage by those who knew him.

"I'm sorry about your loss," I said. Somehow my recollection of that article made Thongden just a little bit more credible. "I suppose it was like losing a father."

Thongden shook his head. "It wasn't only that." Again he seemed to hesitate. "I find myself not wanting to overstrain your credulity. I have already gone too far. But I know too that you will demand to know anyway." Again that unhappy sigh. "You see—I suffered more than grief. I suffered a deprivation of my essential sustenance."

"How do you mean?"

"When Dr. Nelson stopped thinking of me." His eyes were fixed on me now with a look that seemed to be pleading for credence.

I tried to grasp what he was saying to me. "His thinking about you—that was like your—food?"

"In some sense, yes. Our minds were joined. That is, I was part of his mind. The fact that I had material substance, and that there was distance between us—well—thought knows neither space nor time. But the essential sustaining energy came from him. Without him I knew that I would soon also cease to exist."

Once more I had that sensation of the hair lifting along the back of my neck, as I had first experienced it when Thongden came to my home. If I hadn't begun to believe him, that wouldn't have happened. It was a natural reaction to reality becoming weird and unrecognizable. I didn't realize then that this was Thongden's method—that in order to break down my limited view of reality, he had first to twist reality into strange and unrecognizable shapes. "You mean," I said, whispering now for some reason, "that you never really stopped being a part of him?"

"Yes and no. Our minds always had a certain connection. I usually knew what was in his thoughts when I directed myself that way—owing to that basic connection. But I am also an independent living being. It has to be so, you see."

"But you're starting to form a basic connection now . . . with me?"

"Yes—we've made a start in that direction."

"And does that mean—?"

"You're asking if I now also know what's in your thoughts?"

"Hm—you apparently do."

He shook his head and smiled at me. "Not in the same way. Just faintly, you might say. Has it ever occurred to you, Mr. Schwartz, that we are all—as sentient beings—part of one another? But that's something else. Nelson created me. His thoughts and mine were part of one mind—at least until the time I was spun off into a separate existence. After that, well, I often knew what was in his mind. But not as I did when I was part of him. I know his whole life history until that point— but I know by moment to moment what he experienced from the day he arrived in Gangtok."

"Gangtok? Isn't that in India?"

"Yes—it was where he first met his holiness, Samten Rimpoche. It was where the process first began that led to my creation."

Chapter Five

I had been concerned by the possibility that Thongden could get into my mind and note what was going on there. That turned out not to be the case, at least not to the extent that I could get into his. I don't know why that should have been so, but it was something I discovered during my visit. Even as I was asking about it, I realized that he wanted to tell me the whole story of how he came to be, that he had a profound need to tell me. And I knew that this realization was coming to me directly from his thoughts. If, as he claimed, he wasn't reaching into mine, it may have been because he was deliberately refraining from such an intrusion. He certainly understood that I would have been extremely uncomfortable about it. I believed too strongly, as I was to realize later, in my own solidity and personal impenetrability.

But knowing what was on *his* mind didn't seem very strange to me while it was happening.

"You have plans to return home early this afternoon?" he said to me suddenly.

"Is there any reason why I shouldn't?" I said.

"It would be better all around if you were to hear the whole story from me—as soon as possible. To keep things better on track, as you might say."

"I've got time to listen," I told him. "There's no pressing reason for me to rush back."

"You will need some fuel then for your electrochemical factory," he said, smiling. "Perhaps you would like to send out for a sandwich? It is a long story I have for you, Mr. Schwartz."

There was no way I could have refused. Not when I suspected I was on the verge of a story bigger than anything I had encountered in all seven crowded decades of my existence. I telephoned an order for a couple of sandwiches from a local deli. Thongden suggested I settle on the long couch at the other side of the room, where I could make myself more comfortable while listening to him. And without further ado, he launched into his story.

First he explained that he would offer it all from the point of view of the man who had created him, beginning from the time before he had attained physical reality, when he shared the mind of Everett Nelson. And that time seems to have had its beginnings with Nelson's arrival in Gangtok.

The small principality of Sikkim, of which Gangtok is the capital, had a population of about 135,000 in the middle of the 1940s, Thongden informed me. A protectorate of India, the tiny nation sat in the foothills of the Himalayas, providing a trade route between India and Tibet. Maize, millet, rice, and fruit were the principal products of its peasantry. Gangtok itself was known chiefly for the palatial residence of the maharajah and the Buddhist monastery that sat in the foothills of the mountains. For the rest, there were a few British colonial cottages and a small British-style hotel.

According to Thongden, his personal shared memories began with Nelson's arrival at that hotel, whose name now escaped him. From his description of that early awareness, Everett Nelson was forty-three years old, intense, scholarly looking but nevertheless, like so many British academic explorer types, bronzed, muscular, and beard-less. He dressed in khaki shorts and work shirt, like an anthropolo-gist on a field trip. The hotel room, which Thongden seemed to recall vividly from the moment Nelson began unpacking his single large suitcase, was furnished in an English style consistent with the period around 1935, although Thongden gave few details. He could only tell me that while he was vaguely conscious of Nelson all the way back to the point in Nelson's early childhood where memories disappear, his positive and immediate awareness of Nelson began in that hotel room. It was as though Thongden had his own embryonic beginning on that day. This was the best explanation he could offer me.

Thongden told me he had the sense of a very orderly man stow-ing away the last of the articles from his suitcase while glancing fre-quently at his watch. Then Nelson opened the French windows to the balcony and looked down on the Gangtok street as though he were expecting someone. Almost as soon as he stepped back into the room, there was a knock at the door. Nelson went quickly to open it.

Standing before him was a small, young Tibetan peasant dressed in a long cotton chemise and felt slippers, his shoulder-length black hair parted in the center. A glittering pair of pendant earrings dangled from the long lobes of his ears as he gave Nelson a ceremonial bow to which Nelson responded with a perfunctory one of his own.

"Dr. Nelson? I am Pasang."

"Yes?"

"I am to conduct you to my honored master, Lama Samten, who sends you his greetings." The young man spoke a precise, bookish English, Thongden explained to me as he sat probing his memories. He seemed to have remarkable recall, repeating whole conversations word for word. Either that, or he was doing a little ad-libbing to fill in the gaps. In any case, he presented a clear and credible picture.

"Good," Nelson said. "I'm ready. Where is the lama staying?"

"It is a short walk," Pasang said. "Please follow me." The emissary bowed again and turned to leave. Taking nothing with him, Nelson followed, closing the door behind him.

Thongden seemed deliberately meticulous in providing me with every step that led up to Nelson's meeting with the lama. It was as though elements of very great importance were hidden in the details, which he somehow expected me to ferret out. He mentioned, for instance, that as Nelson and Pasang emerged from the hotel onto the streets of Gangtok, the latter walked slightly ahead of Nelson.

"Did that have some special significance?" I queried dutifully.

Thongden raised his long, fine eyebrows. "It was a mark of special esteem. Already Nelson was being recognized as an important visitor. For Pasang to have walked beside him as an equal would have been demeaning to Nelson. But of course, Nelson himself would not have noticed. He was too excited. He had been preparing for this visit for many years and had an overwhelming sense of walking directly into the heart of his destiny. His karma, you might say, had suddenly become transparent."

"He told you all this?"

Thongden shook his head. "Not a word. I was simply there. I was with him. I was part of his mind, not yet become a separate being. In a way, you can say that until the point when I took on physical characteristics, I *was* Nelson Rimpoche."

"Rimpoche?" I queried.

Thongden shrugged. "I am getting ahead of myself," he admitted. He went on with his story.

Following Pasang through Gangtok's narrow streets was difficult for Nelson, who was a talkative man. He drew alongside his guide after some moments. "Pasang, you were exactly on time. I only arrived an hour before you came. I really hadn't expected such punctuality in the Orient."

"I was not aware of the time of your arrival. I came when Samten Rimpoche sent me." He made no effort to enlarge on this statement and seemed to discourage further conversation. Nelson sighed and fell back behind the young man, accepting silence reluctantly until, after some fifteen minutes of walking, they came to one of those small, solid cottages of the sort built by and reserved for British officials on long-term service in India. A male Indian servant opened the gate and led them up a long path to a small porch from which the front door opened directly into a large vestibule. Pasang guided Nelson to a closed door to the right, where he knocked twice. A voice from within said, "Come in."

Pasang opened the door for Nelson, motioning him to enter. Then, as Nelson stepped across the threshold, the young man turned away down the corridor. Nelson found himself in a room that appeared to be a combination library and study. One entire wall was lined with books. A handsome mahogany desk faced the door a few feet from the bookcases. A couple of overstuffed chairs faced each other near a large window to the right. To the left was a large couch. A coffee table stood within reach of the overstuffed chairs. There was a Gainesborough watercolor on one wall and a number of Indian artifacts scattered about.

Thongden described the room as though he were surveying it, almost like a playwright setting a scene. And in the center of it he placed Samten Rimpoche, who appeared to be a man in his sixties, dressed in a garnet-colored robe along with the tokens of his office as a member of the Dalai Lama's court, his hair cropped short in monkish style. As Nelson entered, he pushed aside some papers on which he'd been working and rose from behind the desk. He moved briskly, his hand extended to greet Nelson with an English-style handshake.

"I trust you had a comfortable journey, Dr. Nelson."

"An exciting journey," Nelson said, startled by the strength of the small hand that lay within his own, "since I had this meeting to look forward to."

The lama offered Nelson a chair and settled into the other one as he said, "I have been looking forward to meeting you too. Especially since I had an opportunity recently to read your very intriguing work on gnostic Christianity. The English official who was kind enough to put this cottage at my disposal happened to have a copy in his library."

Nelson nodded, feeling a flush of pleasure. "Thank you. But that was rather an early effort. I'm afraid I wouldn't subscribe today to some of the opinions I expressed at that time."

The lama's dark eyes surveyed Nelson for a quiet moment. "Nevertheless, I was most impressed with your approach to esoteric religious values. The work, early though it may be, still points to an understanding that goes beyond mere scholarship."

"That's most gracious of you, but—"

"It is not meant as praise but as—recognition," Samten Rimpoche said pointedly.

Nelson shifted forward on his chair. "Unfortunately, until now I've only been able to study fossilized cultures—where the actual practice of mystic doctrines has died out."

The lama smiled suddenly. "Yet I've heard you've done much to revive interest in them."

Nelson smiled back. "Oh—I've stirred up a few minor academic storms. But no real victories to speak of. You see—where there is no living relationship to the unseen forces that exist in nature, such matters still tend to be relegated to the suspect domains of magic and superstition. In Tibet, I hope to find evidence from living exemplars to bring to the West."

Lama Samten frowned and clasped his hands together within the sleeves of his robe. His voice had taken on a deeper, somber tone. "But Dr. Nelson—do you fully understand the implications of such an undertaking?"

"I suspect," Nelson said lightly, "that you're about to warn me it might be dangerous."

"More than that. What I'm proposing is that you can't stand outside a living tradition and report on it. It means involving yourself. It also means coming to grips with forces that will be new to you. How well prepared do you consider yourself?"

At this point something strange happened to Nelson. He was sitting there facing Samten Rimpoche. But at the same time he was in another room, obviously a kitchen, listening to a conversation between Pasang and an elderly Indian servant who was readying a tea service. And as clearly as though he were standing next to Pasang, Nelson heard the young man say to the woman, "Are you taking that in to the foreigner?"

"Rimpoche says he is not truly a foreigner," she replied.

"What does that mean? Of course he's a *piling*."

"If Rimpoche says he is not, who are you to say he is?"

"Rimpoche never said anything of the sort to you."

"I never said he did. I overheard him talking to the monk who brought him the letter from England the other day."

"What else did you overhear?"

"Why should I tell you?"

"You're a silly old woman. Give me that tray. I'll take it in. Maybe I'll find out who the stranger is."

Nelson then observed Pasang take the tray from the maid and start down the corridor to the study. And in the next instant he was aware of himself sitting on that big overstuffed chair and listening to Samten, who was saying, "I think your best course would be to begin with a visit to the great lamasery at Gyo-ling-pa. I can arrange for you—"

"Excuse me, Rimpoche, but I just had the strangest sensation of—"

"Yes," the lama said, his eyebrows raised slightly. "As I said, you will be coming to grips with forces new to you. But no matter. I was about to suggest that you start your journey to Gyo-ling-pa tomorrow morning. Are you prepared to leave that soon?"

"Yes—yes, of course. Was it then a demonstration—since I seemed to be in two places—"

By now Pasang had entered with the tea tray and set out a pair of small cups along with the rest of the tea service. After placing the tea cart between the two men and having no reason for lingering, he left.

"You will understand better as you go along, I'm sure," the lama said in answer to Nelson's unfinished question. "You'll be ready then to leave tomorrow morning?"

"Oh yes. Since I already have Lhasa's permission to enter Tibet, the sooner I start, the better. How far is the lamasery?"

"About a week's march through the mountains." Lama Samten picked up one of the small earthenware servers. "Do you care for milk?"

Nelson nodded. "Please."

As the lama poured the milk into Nelson's cup, he remarked, "This may be your last taste of English-style tea for some time. I hope the buttered tea we Tibetans favor will prove more palatable to you than it is to most Westerners."

"I find I have a talent for adjusting my palate to the requirement of strange environments. I hope I prove as facile in adjusting my mind."

The lama sat back and studied Nelson thoughtfully as though assessing him afresh. "Tell me, Dr. Nelson, isn't there something else behind your interest in Tibet? Something more personal?"

The question took Nelson by surprise. "I'm not sure I understand you."

Lama Samten had been holding his teacup to his lips with both hands as he sipped from it in Tibetan fashion. Now he lowered the cup to the tray. "Men like yourself are rarely moved to extreme actions by mere scholarly interests. A sense of mission such as yours usually has something less specific—and much larger—behind it."

Nelson had an uncanny feeling that the lama had looked into the depths of his soul. Yet he was not sure whether he entirely understood what the Tibetan was seeking. He got to his feet and moved across the room toward the window, calling back over his shoulder,

"I can't deny that I find your insight rather startling. Yes—there is something. I wouldn't normally mention it because it's so subjective. But if you'd care to hear about it—"

'Yes, I would," Samten said.

Nelson turned from the window and stood behind the chair he had just vacated. "Shortly after beginning my Tibetan language studies—I was in Switzerland at the time, at the suggestion of my mentor and teacher, Dr. Evans-Wentz. I suppose you know there's a small Tibetan colony in that nation whose mountains so resemble yours. Anyway, I had this strange dream. It was one that recurred several times. The first occasion was at home in my bedroom. I had a charming rented house in a typical mountain village not too many kilometers outside Zurich. I remember awakening and sitting up in bed to stare at the cowled figure of a Tibetan monk standing silently with folded arms at the foot of the bed, watching me. I remember reaching out toward the figure, but as I did so, it simply dissolved. What's strange about it was the fact that I don't recall going back to sleep again. I just continued sitting up in bed like that, for how long I cannot say, until I became aware of the light of dawn seeping in through the window. By then I was fantastically tired, so I lay down and slept until almost noon.

"As I said, the dream recurred several times at different places I was staying, although the dream itself was mostly the same. On the last occasion I was somewhere in Cornwall on a field expedition—where I had been trying without success to contact an alleged faery seer—again retracing a path that had been blazed by Evans-Wentz." Nelson paused, gripping the back of his chair.

Samten nodded in encouragement. "I've read your two papers on the traditions involving the faery folk," he said. "I was naturally curious once I received your request for a meeting. Very discerning, those studies of yours."

"Thank you. But on this occasion, while the so-called faery seer never turned up, the monk did. I awoke one night and saw him standing at the foot of my bed. Even though by then he had become an old familiar of my sleep, I experienced the same sense of fear and nervous anticipation that always accompanied this particular dream. But even then I didn't concern myself too much over it until one morning in the British Museum, as I pored over a rather pedestrian work by a British mountain climber who had lost his way in the Himalayas around the turn of the century, I came across an illustration the man had made—he was, it appeared, quite a competent illustrator. It was a pen-and-ink drawing of the same monk, the one from my dreams, standing exactly as he had always appeared to me, with folded arms. It was clearly and unmistakably he. And beneath the drawing was the caption, 'Tonka from a Tibetan meditation scroll.'"

Nelson broke off and looked expectantly at Lama Samten as though awaiting some comment from him. But Samten remained silent, merely nodding for Nelson to continue. The latter released his grip on the chair back and resumed his seat facing Samten.

"The whole experience," Nelson continued, "up to the moment of finding that drawing in the library pointed to a profound connection of some sort between myself and Tibet. It's hard to express. I think of words like 'affinity' or the Buddhist word 'dharma,' which we would translate as 'calling'—and in fact, something was calling to me. Not just to the scholar in me but to my very soul, if you like. I knew I had to come to Tibet."

Samten maintained his silence a few moments longer. Then he rose from his chair. Standing beside it and looking down at his guest, he said, "Obviously your vocation, or dharma, if you like, has already led you to some significant breaching of psychic barriers." He looked very solemn as he continued. "But I must warn you that such sensitivity will make you all the more susceptible to the psychic influences in Tibet. You must exercise the utmost care. I cannot stress that too strongly. When you encounter new and unfamiliar forces, as you certainly will, you must be ready for them. Perhaps that readiness can be reinforced at the Gyo-ling-pa monastery. It is most important that you go there first before undertaking anything else."

Nelson got to his feet. "I would not have come here for your advice if I had any intention of not relying on it," he said. "I'm grateful for the time you have taken to see me."

"Perhaps," Samten said, "the time will come when that will be reversed—when I—and perhaps Tibet itself—will be grateful to you."

Chapter Six

From the hilltop their horses had just climbed Nelson and Pasang could look back and see the city of Gangtok glittering small and bright in the sunlight, a cluster of low-roofed buildings bunched together like a tiny organic outcropping at the foot of the towering mountain ranges that lay ahead. Both men were dressed more warmly now, wearing short coats with hoods thrown back over their shoulders. A heavily loaded pack mule led by Pasang contained the supplies needed for their slow, difficult journey.

After gazing back at Gangtok for some moments, Nelson wheeled his horse about, and he and Pasang began their journey in earnest. For a long time they rode silently, side by side where the trail was wide enough and with Pasang leading the mule by a long rope. By midday they were moving through a vast meadow that sloped upward toward the high elevations beyond. For some time during the trek, Nelson had noticed that Pasang was stealing thoughtful glances at him. It provided an opportunity to break a silence that had gone on too long.

"You keep looking at me in a strange way, Pasang. Does something about me trouble you?"

"You are a *piling*—are you not, Kushab?"

Nelson, recalling the conversation between Pasang and the serving woman he had mysteriously overheard in the kitchen, smiled. "Well—certainly I'm a foreigner."

"Not that you don't look like a foreigner. And even though you speak our language well, it is still in the style of a foreigner," Pasang commented thoughtfully. Both were speaking Tibetan now as though by mutual agreement.

"Then why do you ask?"

Pasang shrugged. "It was something I heard from Rimpoche's servant. But she is a foolish old woman."

Nelson, pretending he had not overheard the conversation, queried, "What was it you heard?"

"She said you are not a foreigner"

"Perhaps she was teasing you."

"No—she said she overheard Rimpoche say so."

"I can't imagine why he would think that," Nelson admitted truthfully.

"Naturally it surprised her. So she asked me about it. Because I am more educated than she."

"She must have misunderstood Samten Rimpoche."

"I'm glad to hear you say that, Kushab. Because that was also my opinion."

They fell again into silence, except for occasional comments about the terrain, which was becoming more difficult as the ascent grew steeper and the trail more rocky and narrow. Each was occupied with his own private thoughts. Later in the afternoon they stopped and ate from their store of prepared food, since there was no time to make a fire. Pasang was anxious to reach a certain point in the mountains before dark, where he knew of a sheltered spot to set up their tent for the night.

Their destination turned out to be well above the snow line. As they struggled to set up the heavy tent on one of the few bare patches of windswept ground they could find, Nelson remarked that it might have been better if they'd brought a modern canvas tent, which would have been lighter for the mule to carry and easier to set up.

"Only a tent of yak skins such as this can stand against the winds and keep out the cold of the higher altitudes," Pasang said. "You will see, Kushab."

Later, exhausted by the long day's trek and the struggle to set up the tent, Nelson fell into a deep sleep troubled by strange dreams. He found himself wandering through a bizarre, twisted landscape in which the shapes of rocks and trees and shrubs kept changing, their variegated surfaces turning into harsh, demonic faces from which howling sounds came forth. After one such prolonged shriek, Nelson sat up suddenly in his sleeping bag.

"What was that?"

Pasang was also sitting up, wide-eyed with fear. "The voice of a demon."

"Nonsense. Some sort of wild beast. Tibetan wolves, maybe?"

"I know of no wild beast that makes such a sound," Pasang whispered, a thin quaver in his voice. "Besides, we are not far from the cave of *gomchen* Kongpo."

"*Gomchen* Kongpo is a very famous hermit and is said to control many demons with his magic powers. Once before when I camped in this place, I heard that same cry."

Nelson, fully awake now, smiled. "Have you ever seen a demon, Pasang?"

"Once—when I was a small boy."

"But not since you have grown?"

"No."

"This *gomchen*—how far from here is his cave?"

"At the foot of the next great hill," Pasang said, pointing straight ahead toward the sealed tent opening. "Across the ravine."

"In the morning I should like you to take me there to meet the *gomchen*."

Pasang shook his head. "It is impossible. *Gomchen* Kongpo will see no one. Besides, we could not get near the cave without the demons tearing us to pieces."

"If you will tell me the way, I'll go myself in the morning. The demons will not harm me."

Again a stubborn shake of the head from Pasang. "There is still no way to cross the ravine to the cave."

"Then how did the *gomchen* reach the cave?"

"The demons carried him across," Pasang said flatly.

Nelson stared at his young guide for a moment. Then, sighing, he snuggled down again into his sleeping bag. The howling sounds followed him distantly into his sleep, but they no longer troubled him. He was certain now that they were the cries of wolves.

Chapter Seven

"Of course, Mr. Schwartz," Thongden said, suddenly interrupting his narrative, "you must have noticed what has been happening to me?"

"What do you mean?" I said, puzzled and somewhat startled. I had to make an effort to come back to that room in that brownstone building in upper Manhattan. Thongden's telling of Nelson's first experiences in Tibet had been so hypnotic that I'd not only lost track of time but, for a moment, I'd even forgotten where I was.

"You didn't notice?" Thongden insisted.

"Notice what?" I said. "I'm afraid you had me so entranced with your story, I didn't notice much of anything except those paths in the Himalayas you had Nelson traveling over."

"Well—good, then," Thongden said, relaxing a bit. "You see, I was getting carried away myself. After all, it's my story—but in an especially vivid way because when it happened, as I said, I was Nelson, but as I tell it I'm Thongden. It's like being pulled out of myself going over all those details—becoming him again. Maybe I've been getting trapped in too much detail. I should skip through to the main points."

"The devil's in the details," I asserted. "Don't leave anything out. I want the whole story. Especially how you think all this connects with Superman. Isn't that the pièce de résistance?"

"Yes—but you must be patient."

"If you say so."

"You haven't had enough for one day?"

"I've got all the time in the world—for something like this. Especially now that we're into all this, I ought to tell you that—on reflection—there was a certain amount of unfinished business in my walking away from Superman thirty-five years ago. But I can't quite put my finger on it."

The amber eyes glistened with satisfaction. The long, flat face broke into a grin. "Good," Thongden said. "Then I have your interest."

"You sure have. What happened next?"

"We had breakfast the next morning, of course. Pasang gathered some wood, we made a fire, and—well—I had buttered tea for the first time in my life—using rancid yak butter. "I—" He broke off again. "There—you see? Did you notice? I spoke of Nelson in the first person. Because, you see, it was happening to me. Me as Nelson. I had no separate existence as yet."

"Does that bother you?"

"The only point of a separate existence," Thongden explained, "is to focus on minute details. Like using a microscope instead of a telescope. But in Mahayana Buddhism, a separate existence is intermittent. It has no essential reality. For now, let me go on and tell it as it comes. There is much to cover."

I nodded a quiet assent.

"The next thing that happened was as strange as anything I've described so far."

He proceeded to narrate how Nelson and Pasang got off to an early start after breakfast and went high enough up the mountain to be in an area already blanketed by snow, with more falling intermittently through the morning. As he spoke, Thongden sometimes referred to Nelson in the third person and sometimes lapsed into the first person. Finally he told me how the falling snow obscured the trail, forcing Nelson and Pasang to lead their animals on foot around a succession of rocky promontories as Pasang struggled to identify familiar landmarks.

Pasang was getting concerned. "We must find the pass," he explained. "It is here somewhere. And once on the other side, it will be easier. But in this storm I am not sure now whether we go right or left." He paused thoughtfully, making an effort to recall past journeys. "I think—left," he said finally, pointing.

"No—no—to the right," Nelson said suddenly with great conviction. He pointed in the opposite direction. That way to the pass. I'm sure of it." As he spoke, Nelson proceeded to lead his horse in the direction he'd indicated while a surprised and puzzled Pasang followed uncertainly after him.

They went on like that for perhaps thirty minutes. The snowfall was rapidly becoming heavier. Soon visibility was reduced to a few meters. And then they came to a cleft in the high rock barrier. Nelson turned directly into it without a word, moving like a man who knew exactly where he was going.

As they proceeded, the walls of rock rising steeply on each side of the cleft diminished the snowfall and restored a kind of twilight visibility. The passage was barely wide enough to accommodate the tiny caravan except as they moved in single file. And then, suddenly, they emerged from the constricted gorge and found themselves gazing across a long downslope into a broad, flat meadow broken by low, rocky hillocks. On this side of the mountain, it seemed as though winter had not yet arrived, it was distinctly warmer, and the sere ground was marked only by occasional small snow patches. At the point where they stood were a number of rock cairns supporting little flags left by pilgrims. As though completely forgetting the confidence with which he had taken this path, Nelson remarked,

"It's amazing—on this side it's like a different world. I suppose the mountain acts as a weather barrier, shielding the plain." Then he noticed his companion adding stones to one of the cairns.

"Why are you doing that, Pasang?"

"We must make our offering to the gods for our safe journey through the pass, Kushab." He placed a few more stones, then turned to Nelson. "You have never been this way before, Kushab?"

"No—never before."

"Yet you knew the right way to the pass."

Nelson looked thoughtfully back toward the pass. "I suppose—" He hesitated.

"You suppose what, Kushab?"

"I suppose I sensed it from the arrangement of the land."

"With the snow lowering a curtain before our eyes?"

Nelson shrugged in dismissal. "I've traveled though mountains before, Pasang."

As Thongden went on with his long, hypnotic narrative, I once more lost track of where I was. But now, with a mere shift in tone that had the effect of abruptly distancing me from those scenes with Nelson, Thongden managed to draw my awareness back again to that room where the late afternoon shadows had already staked a claim on the daylight while he sat across from me in that natty business suit, watching me intently.

I began stretching on the couch to ease the stiffness. Then I yawned.

"You are tired," Thongden said. "It's been a long afternoon."

"Oh no—not at all. A little too much sitting in one position, perhaps. But I want to hear it all," I insisted.

"Probably I am still dwelling on too many details. I will try to stay with the highlights. But one important thing I do not want to leave out—we came to a village—just a small community of herdsmen. The women and children came running from their tents to greet us. Also the dogs. Tibetan dogs have an addiction to loud barking. The world's noisiest. So—here we got fresh supplies, barley meal, or *tampa,* yak butter for our tea. And we exchanged our animals—our mule and horses for yaks. Much better than horses for negotiating the high mountains after crossing the long meadow. Then, after much friendly chatter and many good wishes, we set out across the meadow, and by nightfall we set up camp just at the foot of another great mountain not far ahead of us."

"You're back in the first person again," I commented.

Thongden nodded and without changing expression managed to shift gears and reshape his narrative in the third person.

It had grown cold again and Pasang made a fire of yak dung—a priceless substance in altitudes where wood is almost nonexistent. There was bright moonlight, and Nelson and Pasang, having eaten, were sitting by the fire before retiring into their tent. The animals were tethered nearby. Suddenly Nelson was startled by a strange sound, hoarse and piercing, that seemed to come from the nearby foothills.

"What's that?" he asked.

Pasang listened for a moment. "A *kangling*—a bone trumpet used during the *Chod* ceremony." He began to rub his hands over his face in a strange, nervous gesture.

"Oh yes," Nelson said. "I remember reading about the *Chod* rite."

Pasang got to his feet. "This place is a poor choice for our camp, Kushab."

"Why?"

The young man shook his head. "When a *narjolpa* is performing the *Chod,* it is better not to be so close."

"What's there to be afraid of?" Again Nelson's Western skepticism came to the surface.

"During the dance," Pasang began, "the sorcerer calls up demons—"

"More demons? Surely, Pasang, you can't—"

"—demons he controls by his great yogic powers," Pasang insisted. "If anything distracts him, the demons can tear him apart— or even run wild through the countryside."

It was early in the journey, yet Nelson was proving to be rather an impulsive man. As the cries of the *Chod* dancer continued, he got to his feet and looked toward their source in the nearby hills. "I must have a closer look," he said.

Pasang gazed up at him in alarm. Then he was on his feet, seizing Nelson's arm. "No," he pleaded. "Rimpoche will be angry with me if you're harmed."

Nelson gently released his arm. "Wait here, Pasang. I'll be all right." He drew his heavy anorak around him, put the hood over his head, and started quickly away from the campsite, following the mysterious sounds. Working his way carefully toward the top of a hill, he came upon a crevasse from which the sounds of the *kangling* emerged highly amplified. He slipped between the jagged walls of the opening to a small ledge that placed him on a level with a plateau ringed by hills. There he discovered his quarry, a tall, ragged *narjolpa* in a garnet-colored, plaited skirt, a yellow chemise with wide sleeves, and a red sleeveless waistcoat of distinctly Chinese design. Over all this was an open monastic toga whose folds imparted a majestic character to the movements of the tall, emaciated monk. The *narjolpa* now repeated in a soft singsong, barely intelligible, a mantra of praise that Nelson recognized, having come across it in his studies. To the right of the preoccupied sorcerer-monk, Nelson observed a small cotton tent on whose sides were sewn words from the Tibetan language, seed syllables of deep symbolic import, as he had come to understand them.

As Nelson lay watching, careful to avoid being seen, he observed the *narjolpa* taking slow, rhythmic steps to the beat of the human skull drum, the *damaru,* which he held in his left hand while striking it with the trumpet, the *kangling* whose sounds had first attracted

Nelson. The strange object was made of what appeared to be a long piece of bone, which, he learned later, was in fact a human femur.

Nelson could not recall exactly how long he remained like that, watching and listening, but after a time he began to feel puzzled and confused, as though the sights and sounds that confronted him induced stimuli that went far beyond the visual. He felt himself almost part of the ceremony and was startled to discover his own hand beating time to the *damaru* with such vigor against the rocky floor on which he lay concealed that small cuts and abrasions formed on the bottom of his closed fist. Then the moon-bright scene began to play tricks on his vision in a way that gave the darker shadows along the edges of the plateau a kind of independence so that they resembled shifting holes of blackness against the velvet fabric of the night. Soon they began to change in size and break up into multiple positions as they swarmed about the dancing figure of the *narjolpa*. Nelson, helplessly fixated now by their erratic and unpredictable movements, continued inadvertently to beat time to the rhythms of the *damaru*. Gradually the pace of the monk's dance accelerated as he proceeded to cry out, "I trample down the self, the gods, and the demons . . ." while turning ceremoniously toward each of the four quarters.

"I trample down the demon of anger; I trample down the demon of lust; I trample down . . ." And slowly Nelson got to his feet, his whole being gradually drawn into the frenzy of the dance. Soon his feet began to move in a synchronous rhythm of their own. After some moments, as though the sights and sounds had awakened ancient spasms of memory that seized his limbs, he felt himself drawn from his hiding place. And finally he found himself caught up in a kind of corybantic paroxysm—his mouth twisting, his face contorted, his hands flailing in a strangely accented response to the living shadows that now rushed upon him from the place where they had been circling the *narjolpa*.

Nelson was no longer aware of where he was or how he'd gotten there. He felt himself moving in and out of darkness. And he knew that his feet, still trapped in the rhythms of the dance, were moving, carrying him off while the sounds of the *Chod* ceremony faded into the night. For a long time the sensation of walking continued, the diminishing beat of the *damaru* somehow still timing his movements. After many hours it seemed to be growing less dark. There was a meadow, and he felt himself floating across it. And then there was nothing at all.

"Are you all right, Kushab?"

Nelson awakened. He recognized the anxious features of Pasang bending over him as he lay on his back on a hummock of dry grass. A robe had been thrown over him.

He sat up slowly and looked around. He was back at their campsite, but the tent was down, the animals were all packed, and the sun was high overhead. Pasang, crouching over him, was holding a steaming bowl of tea in his hands.

"It is already midday, Kushab. We must be on our way."

Nelson took the bowl with a murmured thanks, realizing suddenly that his mouth was very dry.

"How did I get back here?" he asked.

"I cannot say," Pasang replied, sounding troubled.

Nelson sipped deeply of the tea but said nothing more.

"Are you rested enough to travel?" Pasang asked.

Nelson sighed, sipped once more at the tea. Then he nodded. "I'm fine, Pasang."

It was only after they had mounted their yaks and traveled about a mile beyond their campsite that Pasang broke his silence. "You were away a long time last night," he said tentatively.

Nelson remained thoughtful and silent.

After a few more moments Pasang tried again. "I was afraid, Kushab. I thought you would never return."

Nelson stared reflectively back at the hills behind them. "It was reckless of me," he murmured in a low voice. "Very reckless."

Chapter Eight

"But they weren't demons," I said. "I mean—not *really* demons." I leaned forward in my chair, trying to reconstruct Thongden's features out of the twilight that had crept into the room. We had both been so mesmerized by the story he was telling—he with his recollections and I in sheer wonder—that until this moment we had ignored the growing darkness. But now Thongden reached over and switched on the small lamp on his desk. And suddenly he was before me again and not just a voice emerging from the shadows.

"Not demons? But indeed they were. How could they not have been?"

"But really, this is the twentieth century—"

Thongden responded with a low, feathery laugh. "Only right here is it such a century. But what you call the twentieth century, Mr. Schwartz, is only an atmosphere—or a climate. It does not reach everywhere. The forces that make up each climate are never quite the same. Here in Manhattan—in the urban centers across the country —such forces are differently distributed. What you have here, what your media dwell on, what you confront on your streets, are clusters of violence. Anger, menace, hatred, resentment dwell everywhere. But you do not call them demons even though they bring fire and blood and death. Your science says demons are not real. Since you have no names for them, you cannot call them forth and control them. Instead they control you. They fill the land with fear. But not so the *narjolpa* during the *Chod* rites. That night, at great risk, Nelson learned it is not good to deny the reality of the dark powers." Thongden paused, looking around and then back to me. His expression changed. I watched his eyes bring me into fresh focus. Then suddenly he smiled. "But you know about demons anyway. Wouldn't you say that some of the Superman villains—like the Prankster—were demons? And what about that fifth-dimensional imp, Mxyztplk?"

"But those were—fictional."

"I'm not going to insist that everything fictional has its 'real' counterpart. No—but in relation to Superman—especially your Superman, the split-off, fragmented beings that were his villains shared a certain archetypal reality with the one you call the Man of Steel."

"I'm afraid you're way ahead of me, Mr. Thongden." I realized it was the first time today that I had addressed him directly by name.

"But it is late. Perhaps we should go on another time."

I got up from my chair and walked toward the tall double windows at the far end of the room, stretching my legs. Peering out, I found myself studying the dark forms of an overgrown garden at the rear of the house. Silhouetted against the dimly lighted windows of the building on the next street, they assumed strange and unfamiliar shapes, as though they were under an enchantment. They mirrored my mood precisely. What was happening was beyond reality, at least any form under which I'd ever experienced it. But as Thongden had said, I was hooked. I had to hear the rest of it, and nothing in the world could possibly have torn me away at that juncture. I asked Thongden for permission to use his phone.

First I called Kay and told her I'd be staying overnight with Thongden. Then I phoned a local deli and ordered some more sandwiches and a large, steaming pot of coffee.

"All right," I told Thongden as I settled back on the couch. "I'm staying in the enchanted castle for as long as it takes."

I had ordered two Reuben sandwiches, which arrived quickly enough. When I offered to share one with Thongden, suggesting that it was a favorite New York delicacy, he smiled and explained that he really had no need, that I was already supplying him with enough of the kind of food he required.

For some moments he watched me tear into my sandwich, noting aloud with some amusement that I seemed ravenously hungry. I confessed it probably had something to do with his detailed narrations of campfire cooking along with the icy weather he was so realistically describing as Nelson and Pasang continued on their way to the monastery at Gyo-ling-pa.

"It wasn't just the cold, or even the snow cutting off visibility," Thongden resumed. "It got a lot worse than that. When they left their last campsite—after Nelson's fearful experience with the *Chod* dancer—the snowfall became so heavy and deep they couldn't go on. Yet to remain where they were, on that broad plain between two sets of hills, would have meant being entombed for perhaps days. And while they could probably have protected themselves by building some sort of snow shelter, if they were trapped for too long their food would run out. At least, that's how it seemed to Nelson."

Thongden noted that Pasang remained unruffled by the situation, informing Nelson that he would never have led him onto that plain if he'd had any concern about being able to reach the safety of the hills ahead.

"And how do you propose to get there?" Nelson said.

"Anyone who is not a *piling* would know," Pasang explained, unable to suppress a tone of superiority. "It is one of the ways we use yaks and the reason we arranged to bring three, since for carrying ourselves and our supplies two would have been sufficient." He instructed Nelson to dismount from his animal, at the same time sliding off the back of his own mount. Then, maneuvering the third yak to a place between the other two and urging Nelson to push in behind the barrier formed by the three beasts, he forced the center yak about half a meter ahead of its fellows. "This one is the strongest," Pasang explained over the biting roar of the wind. He was now yoking the three animals together in a way that constrained the middle one into its advanced position. Then, with a shout, he commanded them to push ahead. Immediately the three yaks plunged their wedge-shaped phalanx into the shoulder-high drifts. Behind them a cleared path slowly began to emerge. "Astounding," Nelson exclaimed, "you've made a living snowplow of them."

"And so," Pasang said triumphantly, "we will manage to reach the hills. We could never have done it with horses. Only the yak has the strength for such a maneuver."

Thongden's recollections of the next few days were hazy and irregular. He described events in bits and pieces as they came to him, first that they managed to reach the safety of the hills, which sheltered them from the storm; then endless hours of trekking across narrow, barely discernible trails; nights when they camped in the open along trails too narrow to set up their heavy tent and kept warm by sleeping close to a small smoldering campfire; then onward again till they found themselves one late afternoon on a high plateau. It was near sunset when Pasang pointed straight down the path they'd been following. There, about a hundred meters beyond, spotlighted by the setting sun at their backs, was the monastery. Built of rock, it stood on the mountainside about 250 meters above the valley. It consisted of a red temple and countless individual cells perched like birds' nests on the rocks.

As they wound down along a road that approached the *gompa* from the left, dusk had already set in. Above the peristyle of the temple hall, young novices, wrapped in togas, were silhouetted against the bright sky in the west like dark, unearthly beings. The travelers could now distinguish more clearly the many low-roofed, whitewashed stone cells around the main flat-roofed temple, or assembly hall, which to Nelson's eyes somehow resembled a vast necropolis. As they drew closer the novices, lifting conches to their lips, suddenly began to blow, each alternately breathing and blowing to produce an uninterrupted bellowing that rose and fell in a series of crescendos that brought the newcomers to a halt as they listened in awe before proceeding.

The fluttering lights of many butter lamps now began to appear in the *tashas,* the ordinary monks' cells. Among these was a more princely, elaborate *garba,* which Pasang pointed out as the residence of the *khempo,* or abbot. The appearance of the newcomers had caused a stir all through the *gompa,* and there was a lot of pattering back and forth and peering out from the monks' cells. Then, as though on a signal, a nun, her head covered by a pointed cap that was part of a long gown, emerged from the *garba* and motioned to Nelson. At a nod from Pasang, Nelson separated from his little caravan to follow her into the *garba.* There, just ahead, the focus of a wide, candlelit space, was the *khempo,* seated on a high-cushioned, straight-backed chair. Nelson noted that he wore the dress of a lama of the Red Hat sect. He was a lean, wizened man of fifty who seemed to be smiling as though everything he saw were a huge secret joke. This time there was no handshake. Nelson, with a slight deferential bow, handed over his letter of introduction from Lama Samten. After thanking the *khempo* for graciously allowing him into his presence, a protocol Nelson had learned before venturing on his journey, he explained, "This letter from Lama Samten explains my purpose in coming here."

The *khempo* held the letter between his small, thin fingers without troubling to look at it. Instead he picked up a little bell and rang it while urging his guest to feel welcome after his arduous journey and assuring him that tea would be served shortly. Nelson noted that the atmosphere was both polite and very formal, rather than cordial.

Now the *khempo* rose from his chair and beckoned his guest to settle on cushions spread out on a pair of long, low benches, where they might sit facing one another. Finally the *khempo* opened the letter and read slowly and without change of expression as a servant in the attire of a nun set down a tea service between the two men. The *khempo,* having finished reading, cleared his throat and sent a whorl of spittle into a golden spittoon standing beside his bench. Nelson started, momentarily disconcerted. The nun, after casting curious glances at him, went out. The *khempo* set the letter aside and, in silence, poured the tea and handed a cup to Nelson. No words were exchanged until each had managed to sip several times at the hot, viscous drink plentifully larded with yak butter.

"You are here," the *khempo* said finally, setting down his cup, "to observe, to study, to acquire knowledge of our ways. That is correct?"

"I couldn't have stated it more clearly," Nelson acknowledged.

"But nothing is clear, Kushab Nelson. You will read our manuscripts and observe our rituals—with what? Can eyes untutored in seeing see more than they have learned to see? Or ears untutored in hearing hear beyond what they have been trained to hear?"

Nelson made a modest gesture of self-deprecation. "Believe me, Khempo Lobsang, I'm only too aware of those shortcomings. In fact, on my way here I had an experience that I still can't sort out in my mind. Several nights ago I witnessed a *Chod* rite in the mountains—" He hesitated, as though reflecting again on the experience.

"Yes—yes?" the *khempo* said impatiently.

"I'm having some difficulty describing the effect it had on me, Khempo. But—it seemed to me that as I watched, I lost all sense of time." There was a growing edge of excitement in Nelson's voice. "It seemed as though each moment were a meeting place for an infinite number of events—as though past, present, and future were—"

"Before you go further," the *khempo* interrupted brusquely, "let me repeat. The instrument of observation has not been trained. I have no interest in your account of an event whose appearance is quite familiar to me."

"But," Nelson pursued, still trapped in his fixation on the experience, "I was more than just a spectator. I was caught up in—"

"Are you asking me for an explanation of the event—or your experience of it?"

"Naturally I was referring to my experience."

"Which you do not understand. So what is there for me to explain? I can deal only with your lack of understanding. That is—not with your ignorance but with its causes."

Nelson was thoroughly taken aback. "I'm afraid that leaves me rather confused, Khempo."

The other's smile suddenly returned. He nodded. "You will soon realize just how much." There was a brief pause while his eyes rested on Nelson's puzzled features. Then he said, "Since, as Lama Samten requested, I am granting you permission to stay on and study our sacred texts, I will also assign a monk to instruct you in exercises that will help develop your mental faculties. They will also help your body become accustomed to our climate."

With that, the interview came to an end. The nun who had first led Nelson into the *garba* reappeared. The *khempo* took her aside and spoke briefly to her. She nodded, then approached Nelson and again gestured for him to follow. She walked several paces ahead, leading him out of the *garba,* then through the narrow, winding streets of the monastery. The light from the small shielded candle she carried blinked like a miniature beacon for Nelson to follow. Behind him a trio of young novices now appeared, carrying all of the personal belongings he had brought. Everything seemed to have been arranged behind his back but with thoroughness and care. Pasang had gone, apparently taking the yaks with him. His mission had been accomplished, and most likely, Nelson thought, he was on his way back to Lama Samten. In typical Western fashion, Nelson would have liked to exchange a few words of farewell, but he also understood that among Tibetans such exchanges were superfluous because they believe that those who met in one lifetime would meet in many subsequent incarnations and would therefore never really be separated.

"Pasang took off—just like that?" I exclaimed. "After that long a journey?"

Thongden shrugged. "My friend, you fasten on such trivial details."

"Maybe so," I said, getting up and yawning as I stretched and moved around. I had grown stiff again with sitting and listening. "But it's such a strange story. And it keeps getting stranger. So I find myself groping for details that give it more—well—reality. Like—a man traveling through all that wild, frigid country and then just turning around and taking off as though he'd just gone for a walk to the corner grocery. Didn't he at least spend the night and rest up first?"

Thongden allowed himself a chuckle. "I see. Your reality. Props, of course. But I didn't think I'd have to put them in. Probably he did go somewhere and rest up for the night. In one of the monks' *tashas*, likely. But since you bring it up, maybe you're getting tired yourself by now?"

I glanced at my watch. It was getting toward midnight, but I wasn't tired. And I was still hooked. "Not in the least. What about you?"

Thongden shrugged. "Now that I've found you, why would I get tired?" Again that dry chuckle. "All right," he said, waving me back to my couch. "Settle down. We'll continue as long as you like."

Chapter Nine

Nelson followed the nun the whole length of that winding street. He saw other monks and nuns peering out at him from the doorways of their *tashas,* their faces emerging like variegated white daubs as the flickering light of many butter lamps held back the night. After some five minutes of walking, the nun brought him to a *tasha* whose door was standing ajar. Entering first, the nun used the tiny candle she'd been carrying to ignite a butter lamp hanging from the ceiling. The three novices then deposited the visitor's things inside and, in complete silence, left with the nun.

Nelson found himself in a small, square room with two large eye-level windows. In the far corner was a small altar with the usual offerings of grain and a couple of icons shaped of wood and a metal that looked like brass. Slowly he began to unpack. He had a number of books with him, which he now placed on a wide stone ledge that ran beneath the windows. Opening a large square canvas, he drew out a small folding table and chair and set them up near one of the windows. In the other corner he noticed a pad over a large chest, which he realized was supposed to serve as a bed. He sat down on it for a moment, shook his head, and proceeded to unpack his army cot. Then he rearranged the cushions along the remaining length of wall and lit the two other butter lamps dangling from the ceiling. The rest of his things he stowed in the chest. The unheated *tasha* was quite cold, so Nelson continued to wear his fur hat and heavy outer garments as he kindled a meager fire of yak dung in the small fireplace alongside the altar.

Leaning over the sparse flames to warm his hands, he became aware of a bell sounding from somewhere outside, striking a special rhythm. Soon the bell's notes were joined by the orchestrated melodies of a pair of oboelike instruments called *gyalings* and a pair of *ragdongs*—a type of Tibetan trumpet—all punctuated by the thump of a species of kettle drum that shook the ground with its thunderous reverberations. Nelson moved to the open doorway of his *tasha*, listening intently now as an assortment of other unknown instruments gradually added their voices in a keening *raga* unfamiliar to his Western ears.

Two unforgettable days later I was back at home and trying my best to answer Kay's questions. We were sitting, as usual, around the big oak table.

"All right," Kay said. "You sat up all night with this Tibetan whatever-he-is—"

"A *tulpa*," I explained. "Now, I don't expect you to believe a word of it, but—"

"I believe it. All of it," Kay announced. But she said it as though she were swallowing something rather disagreeable.

"You don't have to believe it for my sake," I said. "I was exposed to it directly, and I know how strange it was even then. So don't feel you have to—"

"I really do believe it," she insisted. "Oh, I know you can be gullible at times. But you've been into this for two days, and I figure you've looked at it pretty carefully by now. So on your say-so, I'll really believe he's real. Only I don't guarantee I'm going to believe the rest of it—how he got born, for instance."

"If you're with me so far, I think you'll go along."

"I didn't exactly say I was with you," Kay said, as though this last bit of contentiousness allowed her to hold on to a certain minimal level of disapproval.

"All right—settle down. I've got to tell you about it anyway—just to get it off my chest. Who else would I dare talk to about this stuff anyway?"

So I got back to Thongden's story, picking it up at the point where Nelson left his *tasha* to wander around the grounds, following the sound of the musical instruments. He saw other *tasha* doors opening as monks and nuns, emerging from their cells, moved in the direction of the temple entrance. As they removed their felt boots before going inside, they looked at him curiously since, despite his Tibetan traveling clothes, he was obviously a *piling*—a foreigner.

Not quite daring to venture all the way inside, Nelson lingered in the entrance, noting the dress of the odd, shabby crew, their vestments contrasting strongly with the gold brocade vests of the monastery's leading dignitaries and the jeweled cloak and ornate rod of office of the *tsoga chen shalingo,* the *gompa*'s elected ruler.

I had developed a remarkable memory for particulars during some ten years of doing research and documentary film writing after I left comics, so little detail was lost as I repeated Thongden's long, remarkably precise narrative to Kay. Besides, Thongden had a way of putting images into my mind so sharply that it was almost as though I had been there myself—a condition that was not to last beyond the few days it seemed to take for his hypnotic effect on me to wear off. But I was able to describe for Kay the multitude of painted scrolls of countless Buddhas and deities hanging from the high ceiling of the temple, from the galleries, and against the tall pillars. I told her about hosts of other entities, saints, gods, and demons, that Nelson vaguely discerned in the guttering light of the butter lamps on the frescoes decorating the walls.

At the bottom of the great hall, I told her, were the gilded images of former grand lamas and the massive silver and gold reliquaries that contained their ashes or mummified bodies. But above all was that mystical atmosphere that seemed to envelop the monks, of whom there were about two hundred—so that faces, even attitudes, had an idealized appearance. Then, with everyone seated cross-legged and motionless, the three officials, including the *khempo,* on their thrones and the ordinary monks on long benches very low to the floor, the chanting began. It was deep toned, in a slow rhythm, and bells, wailing *gyalings,* thundering *ragdongs,* tiny drums and large ones entered from time to time in accompaniment to the psalmody.

Then, after a time that seemed lost in an endless, meditative silence, Nelson found himself arriving back at his own cell. He made some notes describing his recent experience, then snuffed out his butter lamp and fell asleep on his army cot, still wearing his traveling clothes.

Awakening with the sun, Nelson was sloshing partly frozen water from a basin over his face when there was a knock on the cell door. Before Nelson could answer, a tall monk brusquely entered and roughly announced that the *khempo* had sent him to instruct the newcomer in breathing exercises.

"They are for the purpose of increasing your concentration and improving the condition of your physical and psychic body. You will do as I do and follow the procedures as I show them to you."

The monk, who called himself Sherab, spent some three hours instructing Nelson, then abruptly left. A few minutes later a nun arrived bearing a number of scrolls, which she placed on Nelson's table.

"These are some of the manuscripts Rimpoche thought you would like to examine."

"Ah—yes. Give my thanks to Khempo Lobsang."

Nelson eagerly sat down and started to pore over the manuscripts. He took some notes. But he was feeling restless and distracted. He got up and paced nervously around the small cell. Finally, assuming the lotus position, he started to perform one of his new breathing exercises—a technique of alternate breathing called *nadi-sudi*.

Since he had already been at this the entire morning with his instructor, he was hardly in a normal state when he initiated the exercises on his own. Something seemed to open up in his mind so that, hardly more than moments later, he found himself sitting in a large room, dressed in the costly brocades of an old trading family while obviously being instructed in *nadi-sudi* by an old guru—and he had the sense of having acquired the skill of it over eons of time. And then, just as he was beginning to become aware of himself as a male Tibetan adolescent, the scene changed abruptly and he found himself back on the ledge, once again experiencing the *Chod* rite exactly as he'd witnessed it on the way to the monastery. And once more he found himself repeating the wild dance of the *narjolpa* from his concealed position on the ledge.

Then, just as abruptly, he was back in his cell, where he seemed to become aware of his surroundings again. He felt extremely agitated. Getting up, he stalked quickly outside and hurried down the street. By the time he reached the *garba* of the *khempo* where he'd first been received the night before, he was distraught. He stood in the open doorway and saw the *khempo* removing a pair of reading glasses from his nose as he looked up from a scroll he'd been examining at the long bench where he sat on a heap of cushions.

"Excuse me for disturbing you, Rimpoche, but—" Nelson hesitated.

"Come inside. Close the door."

Nelson obeyed, then approached and stood over the *khempo* nervously. "It just happened again. I mean—something like what happened to me when I witnessed the *Chod* rite."

"Be seated, Kushab Nelson."

Nelson grabbed a few cushions and prepared a seat for himself on the same bench. "Surely there must be some kind of explanation."

"Be more specific."

"Can these yogic breathing lessons you assigned cause hallucinations?"

"In principle, no. Tell me what happened."

"I began reading those passages from the *Bardo Thodol,* making notes for a possible new translation. But I found some of the ideas confusing. So I decided to try *nadi-sudi* to clear my mind—just as I had been instructed." Nelson got up from his cushions and strolled a few paces from the bench before turning. "Suddenly I seemed to be somewhere else. In a different time and place. I was a boy being taught the same exercises I had learned this morning. Now—this is very important—"

At this point in my narration to Kay, I broke off to tell her, "You know, this wasn't supposed to be word for word. I mean—I thought I'd be giving you the gist of what Thongden told me—kind of creatively filling in the actual dialogue. But it *is* word for word. Somehow I remember it exactly. As though he'd implanted the whole thing in my memory in a single piece. It's weird."

"Don't underestimate yourself," Kay said. "You've always had a remarkable memory."

"Not this good," I said.

"Maybe," Kay said, "given the unique conditions—you've risen to greater heights." She said this with a smile. "Never mind. Go on with your story. We'll worry about your memory later."

"Sure—all right. So—there's Nelson and he's telling the *khempo* about being in a different time and place—as a boy." I picked up the thread of my narrative with Nelson's words.

"It wasn't something I recalled," Nelson told the *khempo.* "It was really happening. And yet—while it was happening I was also outside of it—watching it happen. I was—or I should say, I *am*—a Tibetan in that other life—because the sense of *presentness* was so strong." He hesitated. "Then, all at once, I seemed to be back at the scene of that *Chod* rite I told you about. Only this time I couldn't tell whether I was watching or actually performing the rite myself—while *somebody else* was watching me from behind that ledge." He held out his hands in a supplicating gesture. "What's happening to me, Rimpoche? Did the breathing exercises play any part in this?"

"You are aware," the *khempo* said, "that in Buddhism what we call the self is really a composite of many different consciousnesses."

Thoughtfully, Nelson resumed his seat. "Yes—of course."

"Then it follows that as long as you think of self as an unchanging single entity, it's very disturbing to experience anything that contradicts that idea. This is the meaning of the Buddha's statement that all life is suffering. You have just undergone something that says you are not who you think you are. And you're not prepared for it."

"But why is all this happening now?"

"Now—? This is simply the moment when you happen to be reaping the effects of your long-standing desire to open psychic doors. When else could it happen but now?" he said, putting special emphasis on that last word. "Remember too that here, unlike in the West, there are none of the cultural contrivances that serve to support the notion of a fixed ego."

"But—how am I supposed to handle it? What do I do?"

"It is, on the contrary largely a matter of undoing," the *khempo* said. "The breathing exercises will prepare the way for the practice of deep meditation. Then you can begin to dissolve the thought forms that keep you from seeing clearly. But first you must also understand how opaque thought forms really are. You must begin the dissolution process by first creating your own solid thought forms."

After that the *khempo* rose and dismissed Nelson, I told Kay. "This is a long story. Do you want to hear the rest of it now—or shall we wait till this evening?"

"Of course now. You said you'd tell me how Thongden was born."

"Apparently the gestation period began about six months later," I said. "Because it took six months of meditation and breathing exercises before Nelson was ready to materialize a real form. At the end of six months, the monk who was teaching him said Khempo Lobsang wanted to see him. Nelson lost no time in heading for the *garba.*"

"Didn't anything happen in that six months?"

"I only know what Thongden told me—that it passed in breathing and meditation exercises. Nothing more. But there was quite a surprise waiting for Nelson when he finally stood in front of Khempo Lobsang."

The *khempo* was seated on the same cushioned bench he'd used six months earlier. This time he didn't ask Nelson to sit. Instead he handed Nelson a small tied package.

"In this package is a scroll," he said. "It contains a single drawing. Meditate on it in the manner you have learned. Do so for as long as necessary until you have visualized the figure in the drawing in such complete detail that it comes alive. Do not count the days or the weeks. Learn patience. And when you have succeeded in this project, you are to dissolve the thought exactly as you created it. You will then understand the opacity and reality of thought. And together, Chela Nelson, we can work on dissolving the thought form that you now think of as yourself."

That was all. Nelson was dismissed. He returned quickly to his *tasha,* sat down before his small desk, untied the package, and unrolled the drawing. What he saw made his eyes widen in disbelief. He was staring at the finely drawn figure of a monk, which he recognized instantly. It was an exact rendering of the figure from the recurring dream he had described in detail to Samten Rimpoche back in Gangtok. For some moments he felt as though some kind of psychic trick were being played on him. He sat there silently, wondering whether to give it all up before these Tibetan mind games really began to threaten his sanity. Perhaps, after all, he was too Western to risk further involvement in this strange culture.

There was a knock at the door. Then the monk who had conducted his breathing and meditation lessons appeared. He drew a package from his cloak. It was also a scroll, tightly rolled. "Lobsang Rimpoche instructed me to tell you," the monk said, "that he has chosen three precepts from the work known as the *Supreme Path of the Rosary of Precious Gems.* He requested that you read the three precepts aloud to me. Rimpoche also asked me to transmit any other message you might wish to convey to him after you have read the precepts."

More puzzled than ever, Nelson opened this second scroll, glanced at it quickly, and after some moments of thought, began reading aloud.

"Ideas, being the radiance of the mind, are not to be avoided."

"Thought forms, being the revelry of reality, are not to be avoided."

"That which cometh of itself, being a divine gift, is not to be avoided."

Nelson then rerolled the scroll and handed it back to the monk.

"Thank you, Kushab Nelson."

"Tell Rimpoche," Nelson said with a faint smile, "that I understand the message. Tell him that I will not try to run away from the thought form that pursues me."

The monk bowed briefly, turned, and left the *tasha.*

Chapter Ten

*I am beginning to believe that it may be possible for
an idea, particularly one that is strongly held or gen-
erously housed at an unconscious level, to manifest
its own independent sort of reality.*

—LYALL WATSON[2]

I n Thongden's own words, this was the beginning of his gestation
period. It was the third night in a row I had spent with him. Kay
was very understanding about my absence. And since I couldn't
just sit and listen to him for twenty-four hours at a stretch, I crashed
on his sofa for a few hours at a time. But the story was so overpowering, or Thongden himself was so overpowering, that I simply had
to hear the rest of it, so I didn't go home. And maybe because I was
caught in a strange state between sleeping and waking, the whole
story became that much more entrancing. If Nelson had been experiencing what he felt were states of lucid dreaming, I was certainly
experiencing something similar, especially as we got deep into the
second night and Thongden began describing in detail how Nelson

began to spend long hours meditating on the image of the monk, which he had tacked up on the wall of his *tasha*.

He would sit in the lotus position, meditating on the image, then interrupt his meditation with brief naps, followed by the taking of some simple nourishment brought in twice daily by one of the nuns. Then he would return to meditating on the image. This process went on for days or weeks. Thongden himself was not sure, except that after a time he seemed to see Nelson as separate from himself—in brief flashes. It was as though he were assuming a kind of faint phantasmal shape, at first only for seconds at a time. But long enough to notice that he could look down at a body of some sort, seeing chest, stomach, hands, and feet that were his except that they lacked substance. He could see them in outline—transparently—while watching Nelson squatting there in front of him as he, Thongden, stood just in front of the scroll bearing his image that was tacked onto the wall behind him!

"I seemed to flicker on and off," Thongden told me. "But I never really stopped being Nelson at that stage. Probably I was beginning to materialize at a very low level—the way it was when I first came to visit you at your house—I mean, the way it was with Superman."

"Superman?" I repeated, taken aback. "What's Superman got to do with it?"

"Not all the time," Thongden went on, as though he hadn't heard my question. "But frequently enough. The image was certainly present when I first visited your home."

"Superman? That's impossible. How could Superman—?"

He interrupted me with an upraised hand. "The very first time I walked into your kitchen, I saw a faint image of Superman standing over your shoulder, watching you."

I was beginning to get the uncomfortable feeling that Thongden was becoming strangely aberrant. "How come I've never noticed it, then? And why should it be the case anyway? I never meditated on Superman or even dreamed of trying to materialize him."

"Oh—but you did, Mr. Schwartz. Although you wouldn't have described what you were doing in just those words. But for you, Superman was necessarily a mental formation. Such visualizing, whether voluntary or not, involves a buildup of psychic forces. Or perhaps I should call them creations. Like children born of flesh, these mind creations separate their lives from yours, escape your control, and act with an independence entirely their own. Certainly that is my own case. In the case of your Superman, or any other of your visualizations, such independence may have been only partially realized. But it will come in time. You will see."

"Even coming from you, that whole possibility is—well—inconceivable."

"Do you remember the last Superman story you wrote?" he asked unexpectedly.

"Thirty-six years ago?"

"Yes—thirty-six years ago. When you walk out on something you've been doing for nineteen years, you're likely to remember why."

I could feel a sheepish expression stealing over my face. I tried to mask it with a shrug. "Well—actually, I do. You're right."

"Tell me about it," Thongden said.

"Well—it was a story about Superman transferring his powers to Lois Lane," I said readily enough, adding quickly, "but it wasn't my idea."

"No—of course not," Thongden said, nodding. "But why was that a problem? During all those years, you must have had other story ideas you didn't like thrust on you by editors. It wasn't always the writers who came up with the plots."

"You seem to know a lot about it," I said, unable to avoid a faint note of asperity.

Thongden shrugged. "It stands to reason," he said.

"Sure—there were stories I didn't like doing," I admitted. "With most of DC's editors, you could work things out. They also understood the character—what his possibilities were. What he could do and what he couldn't."

Thongden frowned. "Listen to yourself, Mr. Schwartz. Are you saying you couldn't just make Superman do anything you wanted? Why not? Wasn't he just a made-up personality?"

"You're playing games with me, Thongden," I said, addressing him that way for the first time. "You read my article. You know that Superman had grown into a very precisely defined personality over the years—so much so that we had to follow his character as it had developed. Or it wouldn't have been Superman. And then there was Weisinger."

"Weisinger?" Thongden repeated.

"The last editor I worked with on Superman. He was the guy who took over from the one I'd worked with before—Jack Schiff. Weisinger was difficult to work with," I added, expressing by this understatement a truly saintly forbearance.

"Was he a big fat man?" Thongden said suddenly.

I was startled. "Yes—how would you know that?"

"Why—I saw his image too, somewhat fainter than Superman's, and I supposed that—"

This was more than I could accept. So I asked Thongden to describe Weisinger. It turned out that he couldn't. "The image wasn't detailed at all. Much too faint to descry more than an outline," he said. "Look—there's nothing strange about my seeing images around you. Maybe I can explain it in another way. You're familiar with stories about individuals who've gone through the so-called near-death experience—how they frequently see their whole lives pass before them? Well—it's really because of those phantasms everyone carries around. When the outer light grows dim, the inner one becomes brighter. Everyone is surrounded by remnants of old thoughts and the partial materializations that result from them. Thoughts do indeed take on a certain independence—depending on how far they have been materialized, of course. You *know* that happened to me. But—"

"But what?"

"Before getting back to that, let's get this Superman question out of the way. Isn't it the case that you were so angry about writing that last story that you quit—because, from your point of view, it was out of character for Superman to be able to give his powers to Lois Lane?"

"Exactly right," I admitted. "It trivialized Superman."

"That was *your* Superman," Thongden said. "The one you made a mantra of."

"I made a mantra—?" The disbelief was evident in my tone as my voice rose half an octave in protest.

"Now, wait—I'm not saying you did this naively, out of some primitive impulse. Quite the reverse. The philosophical bent that governed you, that was always whispering disdainfully in your ear because you wrote comics to make a living—you compromised with it by giving Superman a kind of philosophical gloss. You began to think of him as a sort of degenerated religious symbol—an avatar for the underprivileged and the dispossessed. All this was in your article. So it was obvious to me that you'd been reflecting quite deeply on Superman. You had indeed made a mantra of him, and in your own way, you did give him a kind of independent reality. That's what Weisinger violated. And that's why you quit. But—it didn't stop there. You had implanted your own philosophical image of Superman so firmly within yourself that it was able to guide you very quickly into a whole new career. Several careers, in fact. I'm sure you could tell me exactly how that happened better than I can."

"All I remember," I said, "was that I walked out, after nineteen years without any training to do anything else. I had a wife and five kids—"

"And your Superman image. That's what made the difference. The way you understood Superman's meaning as an avatar was not very literal. You sensed Superman as the image of something that came into being in the individual in moments of extreme personal crisis. The Superman self, as you believed even then, was not something one could live in all the time. It's a far too heightened level of the personality. Sustaining it for too long could burn one out very quickly, and possibly do the same to those around one. So the Clark Kent everyday personality was a necessary safety valve—a retreat where one could live normally. Of course, the idea came to you from other sources. An early work of Hegel—the greatly admired, greatly misunderstood German philosopher—"

"*The Spirit of Christianity,*" I exclaimed. "How would you know about that?"

Thongden laughed briefly. "You asked me earlier if I could read your mind. I said no. But I can get into many aspects of it. I can recognize influences—especially during these last few days of close contact."

I closed my eyes and seemed to see my old dog-eared Hegel and the passages in which he pointed out that Jesus' miracles were a product of his anger—that Jesus was in such an elevated state that he fairly burned up the countryside with them, not just in destroying the fig tree but even in the cures he wrought—and especially in the Johannine Gospel, where he admonishes a supplicant to pick up his bed and walk and sin no more. To Hegel, it was impossible for Jesus to remain in that kind of state for long without burning up his earthly shell.

I opened my eyes again and noticed that Thongden was smirking at me.

"You went out and stormed the world," he reminded me. "Within weeks, without anything to back you up—you were already past forty—and lacking even the most rudimentary business experience, you managed to get yourself hired into the executive suite of a major corporation—I'll even name it for you. It was a Dun and Bradstreet subsidiary—the Reuben H. Donnelley Corporation. You became a research director there, and you managed to make quite a success of it. In fact, you went on to make about five major career changes after that because you had one powerful image to call on."

I felt a bit embarrassed by such a fulsome description of my activities after leaving the comics world. "Well—there was a lot of luck. I had help from friends—"

"Yes," Thongden said. "You didn't even have a real suit. You had to borrow one from a friend—something several sizes too large for you that your wife had to crudely tailor into something passable—"

"You know too much," I said. But I was smiling now as I recalled those long-gone events. "I guess I had a lot of gall in those days."

"And you had Superman," he insisted.

"I'll never buy into that," I said. "Not quite in those terms."

"Not yet, perhaps," he said. "But you will. You know what I think? We've reached a natural hiatus. You should go home tonight. Sleep in your own bed. Talk to your wife. Then, say, starting tomorrow afternoon, we'll meet here again and talk about my materialization."

It was a good suggestion. I was suddenly feeling very tired. So I took off for northern Westchester and got back shortly after seven o'clock in the evening.

I told Kay the whole story over dinner.

Chapter Eleven

"He really gets into your mind," Kay declared. "It's kind of demonic."

"I've been thinking a lot about that aspect of it," I admitted. "I'm beginning to realize we live in a very strange world, Kay. We pass our everyday lives as though it simply weren't so. But after this experience with Thongden, I find myself remembering all sorts of odd stories I've heard over the years—experiences of friends—things that happened to me—that just have no explanation. We gloss them over."

"What experiences?"

"Remember the Hawaii trip and the *kahuna*? And that stuff I told you about Jackson Pollock's way of painting? And what happened to Marjorie when she short-circuited—and my friend Eric Heilbroner, who could walk into a casino and always win enough to eat for a few days? Well—more and more it seems to me that we get at least half a dozen surprises a day in one way or another. And we never stop to think how they come about. What about the way thoughts unexpectedly pop into your head to solve problems? You ever stop to think about how that happens? Then there are all the alien kidnappings, power points . . . mostly we don't want to focus on such stuff. The world gets too bizarre."

"I think you're stretching things," Kay said. "To make Thongden sound more ordinary. You're trying to reassure me. You think I don't know?"

"What's reassuring about living in such a bizarre world? I mean— he's real, Kay. He's impossible, but he's real. And how many others are there like him floating around? Remember what he said about Alexander Hamilton?"

"I'm sorry," Kay said, "but I don't swallow that one."

"Why not? We know there's a Thongden. How can he be the only one?" I was about to marshal additional arguments when I realized Kay was staring at me speculatively.

"What is it?" I said.

"Well—" She hesitated. We were sitting across from each other at the big round dining table. I had finished my dinner, and my empty plate remained in front of me. I noticed that Kay had barely touched hers.

"Come on," I said. "Out with it."

She pushed her plate aside. "I'm not even sure about Thongden," she announced.

"What do you mean by that?"

"Well—I've never seen him myself."

"Do you think I'm making all this up?"

She reached across and touched my arm. "Oh no. Not deliberately." Looking away, she said, almost offhandedly, "When I was visiting my sister Emily a couple of days ago, I found my old college edition of *Psychological States*. You remember it?"

"No."

"Mostly it deals with hallucinogenic states brought on by drugs. All those LSD experiments in the '70s by psychiatrists like Grof. But there's a chapter on hypnogogic states—self-induced. I just thought—I don't know. First you have this strange visitor who shows up here on a bicycle. Then you go off for days to this mysterious house on upper Broadway where all these mysterious things are happening. And then there's all this stuff about Superman materializing, and Thongden materializing, and I remembered all that research you did on Tibet a few years ago for the National Film Board documentary—"

I was so astonished that for some moments I couldn't find the words to reply. What could I possibly have said? She thought I had gone off the deep end. Finally, in a deliberately controlled voice, I said, "You think I'm crazy? That these are hallucinations?"

"Of course not, Alvin. People get these things—I mean, they happen to perfectly normal people. Sometimes as a result of stress, or some need to make a major life change. A kind of deep cry from the subconscious—"

"Kay—that's a lot of psychological jargon from people who refuse to acknowledge the existence of the paranormal."

"I'm not saying it isn't so," she said a little breathlessly. "I'm not saying it *is* so either. But—I have an idea."

"About what?"

"About Thongden."

"Yes?"

"I'd like to meet him."

"Ah-hh." I exhaled a long, low sound. Before I knew exactly what I was saying, I replied, "Well—of course. I'm sure that can be arranged." As I felt her eyes upon me, I got up from the table, crossed to the kitchen entrance, and plucked the telephone from its wall cradle. "In fact, I'll call him right now."

Kay was still looking at me as I dialed the number and waited while I counted three rings on the line. Then I heard a low, muffled voice "Please leave your message for Mr. Thongden following the single ring. If it is of sufficient importance, he will get back to you." Slowly I recradled the phone.

"It's an answering machine," I said. "I didn't think it would be worth leaving a message." Since Kay was still giving me that quiet, appraising look, I grabbed the phone again and held it out to her. "Here—you dial the number. You'll see."

Mutely she took the phone from my hand. I called off the number. She dialed it and waited. After some moments of listening, Kay restored the phone to the wall.

"No—I don't feel you'll get any return call." She glanced at the kitchen clock. "It's after ten."

"Tell you what," I suggested. "I'll ask him tomorrow if I can bring you with me the following day. Is that all right with you? Are you free on Thursday?"

"I can make sure I'm free," she agreed. From her tone I could tell she wasn't exactly satisfied. But it was the best I could do. I didn't see why Thongden wouldn't help me out by allowing her to meet him. It wasn't even necessary for her to stay for one of our long sessions. All that was necessary was that she see him for herself and know he was real. After that she could take the next train home.

But the following morning, when I arrived at Thongden's and broached the topic, he had a different idea. He himself looked different, having discarded his natty business suit and assumed the simple maroon robe of a Tibetan monk. Even the furnishings were different. On the right side of the room, golden images of fine workmanship rested in glazed shrines flanked by dragons and crowned by multi-colored carved cornices. On the narrow ledge before the images were silver bowls filled with clear water and what I assumed to be butter lamps of burnished silver.

When I walked in from the barren anteroom, Thongden was seated in a canopied seat whose straight back made it impossible to lie down or stretch out. The canopy itself had a seven-colored volant representing the aura of the Buddha, as Thongden would reveal to me later. That I was taken aback by these changes must have been apparent from my expression, but he explained that since this was the day he was to recount his full materialization, he felt that the surroundings should be appropriate, in effect duplicating the local and sensual aspects of the event.

But I didn't allow all this to distract me from the need to convince Kay of Thongden's reality. At the first opportunity I asked if she could come for a while on the following day.

"I don't think it a good idea," Thongden responded. "In fact, it is more important that both of you grasp the basics of this experience than the secondary fact of my—reality, a term I don't feel comfortable with. But don't worry. She will be satisfied, even if not immediately. Later I have some thoughts I'd like you to take back with you. It will not only help her understand—it will provide a new platform of understanding for you as well. But first we must examine the genesis of my own reality. We must see how I became manifest, so to speak, and then we can generalize from that."

I didn't quite know what he was getting at, but I sensed that it would be revealed more fully as he recounted his own materialization. He began by describing again that sense he had of separating from Nelson for mere seconds at a time, during which he could glimpse the other seated in meditation before the scroll of the monk. Almost simultaneously he would be Nelson again, first hearing the sound of felt-slippered footsteps emanating from a point directly between him and the scroll.

"It was a back-and-forth thing," Thongden went on. "I was Nelson, and then I was myself watching Nelson from that same area from which the slippered sound arose. And then—I was Nelson seeing a transparent image of the monk from the scroll standing on that very spot. And there I was again, separate, seeing Nelson's eyes widen as he struggled to his feet, his glance fixed on me in growing wonder. I myself neither wondered nor thought. I was as yet too unformed. I simply recorded my being separate. And then it was gone and I was Nelson again, murmuring to myself, 'I've actually seen it . . . I've created a *tulpa*.'"

Thongden went on to tell how, for the rest of that morning, he was Nelson. He remembered rushing out of the *tasha* and down the main street of the *gompa* until he found the *khempo* once again and excitedly telling him of what was happening. But the *khempo* failed to share Nelson's enthusiasm. In fact, he seemed somewhat disturbed over Nelson's unrestrained excitement.

"Yes, Chela Nelson," he said. "It is a very sure sign. But—you must not let yourself get too attached to the results."

Nelson, in his excitement, was not listening very well. He said, "Of course—it's only a beginning. It'll take time to give it true solidity."

"The important thing is to know when to stop," the *khempo* warned.

"That's hardly a problem right now, Rimpoche. After all, a thought can be dissolved at any time."

"You know that is not really so, Kushab. What else is it that sets such traps for us as our own thoughts?"

Nelson felt himself reluctantly being pulled back to reality. "You're right, Rimpoche. Of course. And I'm grateful for the reminder. Believe me—I'll be careful."

Thongden then told me how Nelson went back to his long hours of meditation before the scroll of the monk. He described how the moments of separation from Nelson grew from seconds to minutes. And over a period of several weeks, each separation brought with it increasing solidity. He was beginning to feel the weight of his new body.

Nelson, in the meantime, had become very friendly with Sherab, who had been instructing him in meditation. From time to time he would steal a few moments from his endless hours of contemplating the scroll and visit Sherab in the monk's dormitory, where they would discuss many things about Tibetan culture that Nelson was anxious to understand. Occasionally Nelson would describe the growing materialization of his *tulpa*. But Sherab made it a point not to share Nelson's fascination with this experience.

"Kushab Nelson," he said, "you have already established that thoughts have a power and reality of their own. The experiment at materialization has realized its purpose. Do you not think it time to abandon it?"

"Not yet," Nelson said. "I have gone only part of the way. It would be wrong to stop now."

A couple of days after this meeting, Thongden said, he again had a sensation of separation from Nelson. But this time it lasted much longer. He remembered watching Nelson, concentrating on the scroll while Thongden stood directly behind him. When Thongden stepped forward into Nelson's field of view, the latter still didn't notice him. Nor could he, looking down, see himself. He was still transparent. At this point Thongden was seized by a sudden impulse to separate himself even further from Nelson. He waited for the flickering to begin—when for a second or two he would be inside Nelson's consciousness, then back in his own separate consciousness. Timing himself to seize the next moment of separation, he moved toward the front wall of the *tasha*. And suddenly he was standing outside on the long street that led to the temple hall. Seconds later he was again one with Nelson, inside the *tasha*. The peculiar divided feeling that resulted did not leave him when he rejoined Nelson. It was as though, now that he had achieved such a broad separation, he maintained an iota of separated consciousness even when he was back again with Nelson. This enabled him to direct himself more consistently so that he found himself able to move his materialized transparent self farther from the *tasha* until, by an overweening lurch of thought that seemed to cloud his already shaky consciousness, he found himself suddenly sitting somewhere inside the temple. But he had no clear notion of exactly where he was—in the temple or back with Nelson. It was as though he were simultaneously in two places. Thongden remembered only that as Nelson, he'd had a sudden impulse to find himself.

Nelson rose from his meditative posture, spurred by a vague feeling of excitement. He put on a heavy anorak and went outside.

More snow had begun to fall and was coming down heavily. Without knowing why, he proceeded directly toward the temple. At the door he brushed himself off and lowered the hood of his anorak before going inside. A single butter lamp was flickering in the long, dark room, shedding just enough light to reveal the shimmering, diaphanous form of Thongden seated among the cushions on Khempo Lobsang's official throne. For some time he gazed at the apparition with a sense of wonder. Then he walked up close to it, peering intently into the flat gossamer features. Thongden seemed to be asleep. At least, he gave no sign of being aware of Nelson's presence.

Suddenly Nelson turned and hurried out. He arrived at another low building, the *lhabrang,* a kind of dormitory for the monks. He mounted the stairway and knocked at the door of one of the apartments. Sherab opened the door.

"Something is wrong, Kushab?"

"No—not at all. But you must come with me to the temple. I must know if you see what I see." He could hardly contain his excitement.

With a worried air, Sherab hastily donned outdoor clothing and accompanied Nelson back to the temple. At the same time Nelson attempted to explain. "Something induced me to go to the temple, you see. And when I got there I saw him—my *tulpa.* Brazenly sitting in Lobsang Rimpoche's chair. I've got to know if you can see him too."

Sherab allowed himself to be led along to the temple while protesting gently. "Whether I can see him or not—it is not good for you to become so emotional over it."

"Don't worry. I'm completely in control of myself. But I have to be sure I'm not having a private hallucination after the long hours of meditation."

They reached the temple doors, and, holding Sherab by the elbow, Nelson pushed his way in. "There," he said, pointing to the far end, illumined by the single butter lamp. Clearly the faint form of the monk was still seated on the chair.

"Kushab, I beg you—" Sherab began.

"Do you see him or not?" He kept drawing Sherab closer to the chair.

"Yes—I see it."

"Clearly?" Nelson said eagerly. "Completely? Tell me what you see. Exactly."

Hesitantly, Sherab said, "It's wearing a gray robe—a cowl—exactly like the drawing but lacking in solidity."

"Yes—yes—we both see the same thing. It's there. Not solid yet—but it won't take much longer to develop that. The important thing is that he's acquired a kind of independence. And that—he's *real*."

"But—our thoughts are always real," Sherab explained. "And they always produce some manifest effect." He fixed his great, luminous eyes on Nelson. "Surely you don't intend to go further with this?"

"Don't you understand, Sherab? I've spent decades trying to prove that mythic forms have substantial existence. If you were from the West like me, you'd realize the tremendous importance of this demonstration of mental power. The world I come from is staggering under a burden of technology—as men grapple with the earth and with each other to resolve the problems of life by shaping a monstrous steel and concrete environment that only destroys nature, stultifies the spirit, and reduces people to desperately competing ideological groups—I—I can't begin to tell you how dreadful it is. And the irony is that here—right in front of me—is the proof that we have it within ourselves to restore the original paradise for which we were created—"

"Kushab Nelson," Sherab interrupted, "if men are already trapped by the consequences of their own thought, what do you solve by showing them a better way to build such traps? Beware. You are becoming too attached to—"

"How can you call it attachment when even my own liberation concerns me less than the welfare of mankind? Was that not the Compassionate One's essential message?"

Stubbornly Sherab shook his head. "I urge you, Kushab. Dissolve the *tulpa*."

Nelson dropped a hand to Sherab's shoulder. "I will. I promise you, I will. But not yet. It isn't yet time."

Sherab stepped back, disengaging himself from Nelson's arm. "I have nothing further to say." There was no anger in his voice, only a kind of remote melancholy. Then he turned and walked quickly from the temple. Nelson watched him go. When the door closed behind him, Nelson shrugged resignedly, turned, and walked closer to his *tulpa*, which still seemed asleep on the *khempo*'s throne. Looking directly at the unformed creature, Nelson spoke softly to it.

"I don't know if you can hear me yet. But—the feeling of seeing you like this. It's as though—as though—I don't know. Can a thought feel? Can you speak? Can you recognize your thinker? Come back to the *tasha*. Do you understand? Come back with me."

Thongden came to himself as soon as Nelson commanded him.

He had been sitting on the *khempo*'s throne, separated from his still solidifying body, his consciousness still with Nelson. But now, following Nelson's command, he felt the separation again, became aware of himself on the throne, rose, and followed Nelson from the temple back to their quarters.

The next period of time was very hazy. Nelson returned to his meditative labors while Thongden, instead of solidifying as Nelson hoped, began to grow more and more separate. He would wander around the *gompa* in his semitranslucent state without quite knowing where he was going, visiting various *tashas*, looking in on activities all over the monastery. He remembered on one occasion walking into the *garba* on a day when the *khempo* was receiving visitors. He did not know it was such a day himself, only that a conversation was taking place between the *khempo* and Sherab that he sensed pertained to himself, and so he listened.

The monk and the *khempo* were walking side by side down the main aisle of the room, speaking directly and without formality.

Thongden began to pay close attention where he lurked unseen in the shadows along the east wall.

"I only tell you this about the *tulpa*, Rimpoche, because you alone have the authority to put an end to it."

"I recognize your concern for Kushab Nelson," Khempo Lobsang replied. "But I will not interfere. Samten Rimpoche himself sent this foreigner to me with the statement that he is not truly a *piling* but may even be a true *tulku*—an image of one of our own that he has not yet come to realize. While I am not so sure, and while I am also concerned over the continued development of this *tulpa*, I cannot interfere unless I am asked."

"But surely you have the authority—"

"Ah—authority. I think, probably, Kushab Nelson will act in time to make my interference unnecessary."

"I do not have much confidence that that will happen," Sherab said, shaking his head worriedly.

Thongden understood that his own dissolution was being discussed. The notion so concerned him that he found himself back with Nelson, again sharing his consciousness. But this whole event was a mere glimmer among many of lesser importance as Thongden seemed to find himself struggling through a haze of confusing images and dreams, drifting back and forth between the clarity of being Nelson and the murkiness of being himself. And then, after what must have been weeks, during which the weather had grown much milder as the melting snow revealed bare patches of ground around the monastery grounds, Thongden experienced a strange new kind of separation from Nelson. It was like a sudden jolt.

He found himself sitting at the table, looking down at his hands. They were solid. They were real hands. He next noted that he had real arms. Looking down at his lap, he saw that it too was solid. And as he bent over to stare at his feet, he observed that they were also solid, attached to solid legs and thighs. He was clothed in the identical monkish garments worn by the image on the scroll. He could feel the cloth of his sleeves. He continued to be aware of Nelson, but in a different way. Nelson was more removed—more *other*. Their shared identity was gone.

Nelson obviously felt it too. He came out of his meditation quickly, turned, and stared for a long time at Thongden. Then slowly, gingerly, he went over and touched him. Somehow this struck Thongden as amusing. He smiled broadly at Nelson, as if to say they had accomplished something special together. But he said nothing. If he had the ability to speak, it was as yet too complex an activity for him to try. So he simply sat there, beaming at Nelson.

"Are you going to sit there grinning at me and not saying a word?" Nelson said, a note of combined eagerness and wonder in his voice.

Slowly Thongden shook his head. Then he got up and moved around the table, studying his feet intently as they carried him forward. Nelson stood watching. He saw Thongden resume his seat again, then reach across the table to where Nelson stood. Next he reached into the pouch formed by Nelson's robe just over his belt and extracted the small bowl that Nelson had learned to carry there in the native manner. Thongden waved the bowl at Nelson.

"You're asking for some tea?" Nelson said. "Is that what you want—tea?"

Still moving in that slow, careful way, as though fearful of damaging some hidden part of himself, Thongden nodded an affirmative.

The teapot was being kept warm on a small fire of yak dung burning slowly on the hearth. Nelson secured it and brought it to the table. "All right, my silent one. If you really want tea, then put your bowl down on the bench so I can pour."

Thongden responded by setting down the bowl. Nelson filled it and added a pat of yak butter. "You don't have to stay silent, you know. You have my permission to speak to me."

Thongden eyed him but remained silent.

"Well?" Nelson said.

Thongden again broke into a simpering smile.

"Well—good—good. A smile is something too. But tell me—what are you smiling at?"

The *tulpa* now thrust an index finger at Nelson, almost touching him as his smile deepened.

"Me? You're smiling at me?"

The *tulpa* gave an affirmative nod.

"But why—tell me why you're smiling at me."

The *tulpa* responded with a shrug but remained silent. As Nelson watched him, Thongden sipped at his tea.

Nelson could no longer restrain his impatience. "You can speak, can't you?"

In response, the *tulpa* set his bowl down, rose from the table, and with folded arms took up a stance directly in front of the scroll bearing his image.

It was now Nelson who shrugged. He began putting on his outerwear. He felt he had to share his excitement with someone else. He would go find Sherab.

"All right," he said, just before stepping outside. "We've been at this for a long time, and I know you're ready to speak. When I come back from my walk in a little while, I'll expect you to speak. Do you understand?"

The *tulpa*, without moving from his position, gave a brief nod. Nelson went out.

Chapter Twelve

I again stayed overnight with Thongden and got the whole story of his materialization and its strange consequences in one session. After that he talked about how complex reality is. He used the word as though it had quotation marks around it. He said reality had many levels of which we in the West knew only a single one. Then he spoke about strong forces and weak forces, almost as if he were lecturing on particle physics. I felt as though my head were stuffed with so many new ideas that I couldn't handle them all at once. I slept deeply on his couch for a few hours. When I awoke Thongden told me that, at our next session, he had plans to take me on an expedition around town.

"But first—go home. Talk to your wife. Tell her about reality." This time he chuckled over the word. "Think you can come back in two days?"

"You have something special in mind?"

"Well," he said cryptically, "that depends on you. It's your reality."

I nodded. "In two days," I agreed. I wasn't quite sure what he meant by *my reality*.

When I got home it was still early afternoon. I found Kay working in her garden at the back of the house. It was mid-September, just beginning to get chilly toward evening. Nothing much was left growing. We'd had the last of our late corn a few days earlier. Some straggly tomatoes were still ripening on the vine, and there were brussels sprouts that would stay on for a month or two into the first snows. Kay wore an old baseball cap to keep the sun from her eyes. She was squatting, cleaning out the dried stalks of one of the old dead rows.

"Did you ask him?" It was the first thing she said as I approached.

"I asked him," I said.

She got up. "Let's go inside!"

I put an arm around her shoulders by way of greeting. "He had a better idea," I said, feeling my way carefully.

She didn't say anything more until we got inside the house, but I could feel her reaction in the stiffening of her shoulders under my fingers.

I sat down on the living room rocker that faced the long, low couch where Kay curled up as though trying to make herself as small as possible.

"You're right," I admitted without waiting for her to say it. "His answer was no. Because he didn't think that would really convince you either. Just seeing him for yourself—that could be some kind of setup, couldn't it?"

"Not likely," she said. "What would you do—have someone dress up like Thongden? That's even crazier."

"Not what I mean," I explained. "You can see the strangest things with your own eyes—and you still might not believe them. It happens all the time. It's the way we are. That's why he thought there was a better way. It'll take a little more time, he said. Are you willing to be patient a little longer?"

"I'll know as I go along," she said. "Are you going to tell me what happened the last couple of days?"

So I went through the whole story of Thongden's materialization and what happened as a result of it. After I got past the part where Nelson ordered Thongden to speak to him when he got back from his visit to Sherab, I described how Nelson, not finding Sherab in his quarters, went for a long walk around the *gompa* and finally, leaving the grounds, headed along a trail toward a nearby mountain. The snow had already melted, and little white flowers were springing up everywhere.

Nelson was feeling a fierce excitement at having achieved such a powerful materialization—full proof that thoughts have the awesome power of creation. He could still feel Thongden's presence in a kind of muffled way, as though their minds were linked, but because they were now separated a certain clarity was gone. The contact was still strong enough for him to sense a determination emanating from Thongden, but he could not tell what it meant.

For a while he sat down on the path, his back against a rock, staring up at the sky and trying to empty his mind. Looking back toward the *gompa,* he noticed a couple of monks hurrying up the path toward him. Beyond them he saw a large group gathering around the main temple.

The first of the two approaching monks drew close. "Kushab Nelson—come quickly."

"What is it? What's happened?" Nelson got hurriedly to his feet.

"Rimpoche wants you at the temple. At once."

Alarmed, Nelson started to run alongside the monks back to the *gompa.*

"What's wrong? Why is everybody standing out there?" he demanded.

"Trouble. You'll see."

They soon entered the exterior temple grounds as the encircling throng of monks and nuns parted to allow Nelson through. Drawing closer, Nelson could now hear through the open doors a loud, booming voice from inside. He hurried in and found the *khempo* and other dignitaries gathered in a group just beyond the entrance.

"What is it, Rimpoche?" Nelson called out over the voice that resonated from the farther end of the great hall.

"See for yourself," the *khempo* said. "Your *tulpa* has taken over the holy seat of the temple."

"Oh—no."

Sherab came alongside Nelson, addressing him angrily. "This is because you did not obey Lobsang Rimpoche's order to dissolve the *tulpa*."

Nelson peered down the long, dimly lit hall toward the tall figure on the *khempo*'s throne. The *tulpa* was waving its arms and shouting. "What is he saying?" Nelson murmured, unable from this distance to distinguish the words through the low-frequency reverberations of the temple.

Another dignitary approached Nelson. "Some of the monks wanted to drag it out, but we feared to desecrate the temple with such a struggle."

Without replying, Nelson started toward the *tulpa*, only to be restrained by Sherab, who grabbed at his coat sleeve. "No—no. Do not rush at him. Sometimes these *tulpa*s have great strength. If you frighten it, it may hurt you, Kushab."

Nelson freed his arm. "He won't hurt me," he said. "Can you understand what he's saying?"

"What does it matter? You must dissolve it—if you can."

"I know—I know," Nelson said with a wave of his hand as he started off again. Walking quickly, he was soon close enough to distinguish the *tulpa*'s words.

"—because I am life and truth. I am the wisdom of wisdoms. . . ."

In another moment he stood facing his own thought-creature as it squatted on the throne. The *tulpa* had picked up the great *dorje* of the *khempo* and was waving it like a club. Feelings of concern mingled with a certain pride of creation as Nelson studied the all-too-solid personality that confronted him, whose great booming voice continued uninterrupted.

"I am the all in all. So do I say to you all. So am I commanded to speak."

"Get down from there," Nelson called out, standing before the throne, his hands thrust forward in a gesture of command. "At once. You're not real. You're only a shadow of my mind. Get down."

Angrily, Nelson reached up to grab it. The *tulpa* burst into shrieks of wild laughter, edging back on the great seat to avoid the outstretched hand.

"Get down. Return to your quarters," Nelson shouted.

In response, the *tulpa* hurled the *dorje* at Nelson. The heavy scepter passed harmlessly over his shoulder as Nelson leaped back in alarm. He remained about five meters from the throne, watching warily, wondering what to do next. Suddenly the *tulpa* leaped down, turned, and ran toward the deeper shadows at the rear of the temple.

For a few seconds the disconcerted Nelson stared at the vanishing figure. Then he started in pursuit. The group of temple dignitaries came up behind him as he raced after the *tulpa*. Their admonishing voices followed him.

"You will never dissolve it by chasing it."

"Kushab Nelson—you are like a dog pursuing his tail. You must stop." It was Sherab.

Then came the softer voice of the *khempo*, addressing not Nelson but his admonishers. "Do not interfere."

"But is it right to let him lend strength to his own folly?"

And then Nelson was too far ahead to hear anymore. He had come to a narrow, squared opening—a short tunnel through the back wall. Ahead of him, bursting into the daylight, was the fleeing *tulpa*. Nelson plunged recklessly after him, emerging at the rear of the temple, which stood on the eastern edge of the *gompa*. Just beyond were the mud huts of a small village, the residences of lowly service workers of the temple and their families. Beyond these Nelson noted a stone-fenced corral surrounding mud-brick stables sheltering horses and yaks. And then he saw the *tulpa,* already mounted on one of the horses and riding out of the village toward the hills beyond.

As I sat listening to Thongden's story in that room just off upper Broadway accoutred with Tibetan artifacts, I felt it hard to believe I was not somewhere in the Himalayas. Obviously Thongden had had a bizarre and difficult materialization, apart from the sheer fact that the materialization itself was bizarre. But I was utterly caught up in every word of his narration.

Thongden explained that because the mental umbilical cord, as he called it, between himself and Nelson had not been fully cut, he was also aware of Nelson's own thoughts and state of mind. Indeed, at some moments he still seemed to be Nelson pursuing himself. At others he was a separate being in fearful flight, running desperately from the threat of being dissolved, not discovering until long after that this pursuit had actually been strengthening him and that Nelson could have far more easily dissolved him if he had remained at the *gompa.*

After a day and a night of riding, he came upon a small village of yak tents, along with a few rude mud-brick houses, set in a sheltered valley. Here the spring was far more advanced than in the hills where the *gompa* was located. There were yaks and horses grazing, dogs running about, and a group of children playing a game with rocks in a meadow alongside the village.

In this meadow, which was separated from the village by a line of large prayer wheels and rows of flags, Thongden abandoned his horse and joined the children. They accepted him unquestioningly as he became part of their game, which was played by moving rocks from place to place on the ground. They would run from one rock to another that had just been repositioned. Thus, the rocks served as mobile bases around which the children formed constantly shifting lines, running back and forth with much gaiety and laughter. The tall *tulpa* ran among them, sharing their laughter as though he had forgotten Nelson's pursuit.

"Of course I hadn't forgotten," Thongden explained to me. "But even though he was pursuing me, I was still with him enough to realize that he had no hostile intention. I knew something was wrong when everyone got so excited about my sounding off in the temple. And when Nelson came after me, I panicked. I really did believe at first that he was going to dissolve me. That's why I ran. For eighteen hours. And then I became involved with the children and realized that everything was going to be all right."

And that was how Nelson found him—playing with the children. Nelson tethered his horse at one of the stone mounds supporting a prayer wheel and waited. After a time, the *tulpa* left the children and walked slowly over to him. The two sat on the ground. And talked.

"I realized as I rode angrily after you through the night that you only did what I asked," Nelson admitted, just as Thongden knew he would.

"I did not understand that speaking was something different from proclaiming," Thongden replied. "That was why I sat on the *khempo*'s throne—to proclaim. I thought it was the proper place."

"I did not use quite the right word. I said the word 'proclaim' for 'speak.' The Tibetan language still confuses me. It was really my fault," Nelson admitted.

"Things cleared up in my mind quite a bit during the night," the *tulpa* confessed. "I realize now that the knowledge I have comes from you. Part of your mind. But it has not all unfolded yet."

"That's another strange word," Nelson said. "'Unfolded'—in the sense of 'manifesting.' It seems to me that the conscious brain is not constructed to grasp what it knows all at once. It really does have to unfold."

"But am I not a problem for you?" the *tulpa* asked. "The *khempo* has ordered you to dissolve me. But you are not obeying."

"I lost the capacity to do that when I started to pursue you. The *khempo* will probably understand that. He knows I am a Westerner.

In the West we relate differently to objects and—" Here Nelson allowed a faint smile to touch his lips. "—I suppose to self-created beings."

"But he will make you confront the problem," the *tulpa* said.

"It's a bigger problem than that," Nelson explained. "My whole purpose here is to learn to dissolve the self I think I am. Not just you. But Everett Nelson as well—by becoming aware that I am simply a composite of many smaller consciousnesses with no essential reality. You—you're just one of those consciousnesses." He broke off, obviously puzzled by his own thoughts. He looked quizzically at the *tulpa*. "Since I'm not going to dissolve you—maybe you should have a name of some sort. What shall I call you?"

"I believe I do have a name. Or my image does—the monk on the scroll. He was called Thongden."

"He was a real person?"

The *tulpa* shrugged. "Are you?"

And Nelson laughed.

"We separated after that meeting," Thongden told me. "We decided it was better that way. Since our minds would remain in touch, we had two separate sources of acquiring knowledge. So Nelson went back to the *gompa* and resumed his studies as a *chela*—a disciple of the *khempo*. In the meantime, the *khempo* too had changed his mind about dissolving me. Something had come up while Nelson was away. The *khempo* had had a visit from a great *gomchen* who explained that I would be needed in the coming dark days for Tibet."

"He foresaw the Chinese invasion?"

Thongden nodded. "I was eventually sent here to advance the Tibetan cause. For some years I have been working with an ad hoc committee to help do just that. There are some important people involved, but because of diplomatic problems it is all unofficial."

"But—what do you do in that work?"

"I listen, I observe, I wait, I work on reports concerning human rights violations against the Tibetan people. Until recently I was fully preoccupied with that. Then—as I told you, Everett Nelson unexpectedly died. I needed another source of support for continuing my work. That was how I found you." He broke off and made a gesture as though he were brushing off stray thoughts with a sweeping movement of his hands. "But I am getting far ahead of myself." His eyes resumed their earlier reminiscent glow.

"I decided to stay in that small village with the children. Since my care was not a problem—I was adequately sustained by remaining in the thoughts of Nelson—the villagers, not having to feed me, were happy to have me remain in close contact with the children. To them I was indeed a simple *tulpa* who would harm no one and, in fact, might even be a true *tulku,* that is, a reincarnation of some learned lama who had come among them to bear gifts of the spirit from which their young ones would surely benefit.

"Of course I was the real beneficiary. To be among children, where reality has not hardened into the fixed forms and limitations of adulthood, was an enriching experience. With them the imagination is free to explore all sorts of wonders and possibilities. The world becomes infinitely plastic and flexible. Limits do not exist."

Thongden then told me several remarkable stories of his life with the children. He explained to me that they could see things, especially when they were away from the village and the eyes of the adults. The stones of the valley floor took on a life of their own. The children insisted they were alive, that they could see pulsing, colorful auras around them. They saw the spirits of the rhododendron bushes that grew at the foot of the nearby mountain. They saw remarkable birds and other kinds of creatures that their parents saw only in dreams. But to the young ones these were not dreams, and they worked hard to teach Thongden to see as they did. Sometimes they succeeded. He glimpsed flickering images from time to time and on a couple of occasions did manage to see a tall being with the head of a man and the beak of a bird clad in multicolored outer garments made of feathers. The image lingered for many seconds before it gradually faded away. The children cheered with excitement when Thongden reported this to them.

One day—Thongden thought that it must have been a long time after he came to the village because he was becoming aware that some of the youngest children were new to the group and some of the oldest had left—they decided to introduce him to their "secret."

Taken by the hand by Dawa, a boy of fourteen, Thongden was led to a hidden place at the foot of the mountain. It was now winter. Snow mantled everything in sight, and since it was a clear, sunny day the children were not only dressed in heavy furs but their faces were smeared with butter and soot to protect them from snowburn. But as they approached the hidden place, which was a narrow pass that led into a sheltered circular formation in the rock, Thongden was astonished to see grass growing. The cold, of course, did not bother him, but when he saw the children removing their warm outer garments and entering the place as though it were summer, he became somewhat alarmed for them.

"You will freeze," he warned them.

They laughed at him. Dawa pointed ahead to where a group of the children were already squatting in a circle around a bare patch of ground. Thongden's young guide took him by the hand and led him toward the circle. "You do not see?" he said.

"See what?" Thongden noticed only that the children were holding their hands out before them, but he could not understand why.

"It is our *kyilkhor*," Dawa explained, using the Tibetan term for secret magic. "It is not something we share with the grown ones. But you are different. You belong to us." He pulled at Thongden's hand and got him to join the circle as the children made room for him.

After some moments Dawa said, "Do you see yet?"

"Only that none of you seems to be cold."

"But you do not see why?"

Thongden shook his head. Dawa nodded. He turned to the others and told them to join hands. The youngsters on either side clasped Thongden's hands, including him in the now closed circle. "Concentrate," Dawa commanded him, "and look toward the center."

Thongden went into a quiet meditative state, which he understood well from his continuing contact with Nelson. He closed his eyes, then opened them. And then he saw it. A great fire was burning away in the center of the circle. It was simply there, feeding on nothing, although it sent out great waves of heat. Suddenly he understood. He smiled happily at the youngsters, and they smiled back. They knew that he knew.

Chapter Thirteen

A s I explained to Kay, Thongden's story had a profound effect on me. Probably it was deliberate on his part because it clarified why he had gone to the trouble to create that magical Tibetan environment in his room. It certainly put me into a susceptible state. When he made that remark about him and the children understanding each other, it broke open a hoard of old memories for me.

First I caught that strong image of the power of childhood imagination. Then I found myself transported back to a scene somewhere around the summer of 1944. I was looking out the window of a rented cottage in Provincetown, where I had decided to hole up while working on a couple of long continuities for the Superman daily newspaper strip. On that particular morning I had bogged down—literally run out of ideas. I was doing a story about two professors, one of whom was a lively and imaginative English specialist, the other a dry-as-dust, by-the-book professor of physics. He was named, accordingly, Professor Duste. It was he who in the beginning of my story flunks one of his students for writing in a term paper that Superman had flown faster than the speed of light. "Absurd and impossible," Duste points out. After all, the claim utterly ignores Einstein's special and general theories of relativity. So why wouldn't a self-respecting physics professor object? But then the student shows up waving a copy of the *Daily Planet* bearing the headline "Superman Flies Faster Than Light." "You see," he tells Duste. "It's true. Superman *can* go faster than light."

But Duste merely sniffs. Unfazed, he tells the student, "In science, we're not interested in truth. For truth, go to the philosophy department." The distinction, which was a subtle one since modern science deals in probabilities, not truths, may have been lost on some readers, but because it was assumed that the dailies were more for an adult audience than the comic books, the editors let it pass unquestioned.

And there I was, stuck with the problem of somehow finding a way to convince Professor Duste that Superman did indeed possess supraphysical powers.

I happened to look out the window of my upstairs room then and saw what many might consider a striking coincidence. Outside, on the main lawn, a group of youngsters all dressed in capes and costumes of the Superman variety were leaping off small ledges and running around on the tips of their toes in an obvious simulacrum of flight. That is, they were playing at flying—like Superman. It was that part of the memory that rose first after Thongden told me about the Tibetan children gathered around the imaginary campfire.

But there wasn't just a single memory attached to that moment. A whole collection of memories was strung together on a single thread. Among them was the image of my own seven-year-old son standing in the living room of the Westchester house with a couple of my guests, having just shown them the various dress-up features of his costume box—a chest full of assorted bits of coats and capes and shoes and hats and other disguise material. One of the adults, a noted psychoanalyst of the day, Dr. Bela Mittelman, who was associated with the Columbia Medical School division of pediatrics, said to my son, "Why do you like to dress up like that?"

Mittelman asked the question because he was trying to prove a point to another of my guests, the explorer and anthropologist Herbert J. Spinden, who had been among the first discoverers of the lost Mayan cities and had done the initial translation of the Mayan Codex.

"So no one will know who I really am," my son replied to Mittelman.

At the time I was rather caught up in the colloquy between the psychoanalyst and the anthropologist. The former was trying to demonstrate by various redoubtable means that my son was trying to hide from the power of the father—an all-out Oedipal approach, solely for the sake of demonstrating that the power of psychoanalysis had injected something new and special into the modern world. But Spinden promptly attacked Mittelman's assertions. He described in detail a number of achievements of the ancient Mayans that were in many ways not only sophisticated by our standards but fully as advanced. He then cited the discovery of penicillin and other antibiotics derived from tree bark. "As for psychology," Spinden proposed in conclusion, "maybe the boy is just trying to explain that he can fly."

Somehow the conversation took a different turn after that, and we all overlooked Spinden's remark. I certainly did—until years later, in Thongden's apartment, when the *tulpa* told of his sojourn with the Tibetan children and the literal power of their thoughts. That was when it all tied together at once. I wasn't just remembering those kids in their capes running around outside my window. I rediscovered them. Or I saw them with different eyes and through a very different kind of mental filter. In Thongden's apartment, as I recalled Spinden's remark years after the fact, I first began to suspect that Spinden had been serious in suggesting that my son really thought he could fly— and that therefore, those kids outside my window had also been flying. But as an adult I couldn't see it because I was viewing it all from a different dimension. Children often do and see things adults can't. As adults, many of us don't even remember things done as children because of that dimensional shift.

This led me to another Thongden-induced memory from the same hoard. I was in my crib, probably not even two years old. It was in the apartment near New York's Central Park that I seemed always to have lived in. I was alone in the room, staring at the large patterns on the lace curtains that covered the windows. I have always remembered staring at them for hours. And there in Thongden's brownstone, I suddenly also remembered how the figures on the curtains started to move. At first they were tiny people, and it amused me to watch them cavort about. It was like looking at a street I had never seen when I was being pushed in my perambulator outside. After a time there would be a shift, and I would be in the curtain. I was part of the street. I was playing with various toys and listening to people as they stopped to talk to me. That was all. I didn't fly. But I remembered with a sudden certainty my actually having been *in* the curtain.

So now I told Thongden how, as I looked through the window at the kids playing in capes and costumes outside, I became a participant. There was no click, no jolt, no sense of change, no feeling of transition. I was there—one of the kids dressed in costume. And I was leaping off a ledge to challenge another caped figure approaching me. But I wasn't leaping. I was flying. And so were the others. We were all flying around each other, exercising our natural powers.

I then asked Thongden's view of the claims of some researchers that this represented a typical out-of-body state. I mentioned that there was even a whole literature adducing endless numbers of cases to support such an out-of-body hypothesis. But Thongden's response was that the body itself is a composite and has no essential reality. A so-called out-of-body state, he said, is no different from any kind of in-body state that incorporates flying or any other unusual abilities. Thongden insisted that one such state is no more likely than another except that there seems to be, in our Western culture at this particular time, a consensus that the nonflying state is the "real" state.

In any case, I told Thongden about the rest of my recollection of that scene between Spinden and Mittelman that had so pointedly brought back Spinden's remark: "Maybe the boy is just trying to explain that he can fly." I mentioned that Spinden, who at that time was well into his midsixties, had been brought up by Indians and was fluent in a number of Indian languages and dialects. In addition, he had translated the Icelandic sagas. In spite of being a Harvard professor, he was probably well equipped to shift to dimensions beyond our own cultural purview.

Thongden seemed very willing to sit and listen to me for a change, so I now proposed a meaning for my son's remark, "So no one will know who I really am," that seemed more pertinent to Spinden's remark. It struck me, now that I'd been exposed to Thongden's ideas, that in Alan's ordinary state, as my son, he would have been earthbound. At least, that's what it seemed he had been trying to express. Nothing very complicated, really. To be able to fly he had to shift to a different state that would not be rejected by his imagination as incapable of flight. Possibly even a different personality—someone more specialized in flying—like Superman.

Another memory followed as I sat talking to Thongden. I recalled the effort I had put into going through a number of textbooks on contemporary physics just so I could add some authenticity to Professor Duste. In the course of that reading I found myself so fascinated that I went way beyond the needs of research and began digging into post-Einsteinian physics, into the complete re-sorting of Einstein's still newly established space-time boundaries. And this pursuit had led to my solving the problem of what to do with Professor Duste to convince him of Superman's powers, since it opened up the possibility of faster-than-light travel and justified the claim of the student Duste had failed.

It happened in two distinct steps. The first was my having seen not too long before an interesting physical experiment that was to lead to one of the most important theoretical developments in quantum physics, as I'll discuss in a moment. But more particularly, it led me into a dimensional shift that involved time itself, posed a new problem for Professor Duste to be skeptical about, and ended up getting Superman in trouble with the FBI. I told Thongden I was talking about the real Superman newspaper strip and the real FBI. "This happened. It wasn't part of any story," I told him.

Thongden sat listening with his chin in his hand, his face expressionless. "Everything happens," he remarked cryptically.

Chapter Fourteen

One weekend, I told Thongden, while I was still working on the Duste script, Kay and I motored up to Montreal to visit family. I explained that Kay herself is Canadian and had moved to the United States following our marriage. Most of her very large family is scattered across the provinces of New Brunswick, Quebec, Alberta, and Ontario. In those years her mother and three sisters lived in Montreal, and somewhere in the course of making the rounds to each one's home that weekend, I turned on the TV—I don't remember whom we were visiting at the time. I only know that the Canadian Broadcasting System was a frequent carrier of BBC programs, and that the one I happened to turn on for an hour or so of idle watching while prolonged family business was going on in another room was a science program.

That program led to many things. Not only for me—but for one soon to be very influential quantum physicist who also watched the program.

As best as I can recall, there was a table on which stood a cylindrical drum. Within the drum was a jar equipped with a large rotating cylinder. The space between the jar and the exterior wall of the cylinder was filled with glycerine, a heavy, viscous, colorless liquid. The experimenter released a single drop of ink onto the surface of the glycerine. The black drop lay there like a single dark eye staring up at the experimenter. Using the handle of a crank attached to an interior shaft of the cylinder, the experimenter began to rotate the glycerine. As it turned slowly round and round, the ink drop first stretched into a long, thin, circular line, then slowly was mixed into the glycerine and disappeared. But then the handle was turned in the reverse direction, and the ink tracing again formed into a long thin line out of nowhere, then gradually resumed its original shape as a single black drop.

Suddenly I saw in that cylinder the image of the entire universe and how each particular in it emerged from the whole and became manifest before being reabsorbed into the whole again. I knew too that nothing was ever lost. The universe was always a single whole, and from time to time each of its infinite number of particulars became manifest. Apparently this was what the distinguished physicist David Bohm saw too when he watched that same program. Over time it was one of the events that stimulated his important and seminal book *Wholeness and the Implicate Order.*

Clearly I had found the resolution of my Superman plot problem. It lay in the universal totality conjured up by the experiment. In other words, a particle could disappear into the whole and then reemerge a moment or possibly even centuries later. Within the matrix, time did not exist. It was not a difficult leap from that concept to the notion that time had no intrinsic reality. And therefore, contrary to Einstein's hypothesis, the speed of light was no longer a real barrier.

The recent Alain Aspect experiments in France had shown that instantaneous signaling between photons separated by great distances is indeed possible, bringing into question the whole speed-of-light barrier. But this discovery is beyond the purview of my story except to help suggest that what I envisioned was also influenced by the fact that I was already thinking about physics and various new physics theories. In any case, out of the universal matrix symbolized by the glycerine in the BBC experiment, I emerged with the idea that I ought to have Superman explain this hypothesis to the hidebound Duste and then step inside a powerful particle accelerator to convince Duste that he was basically indestructible.

In those days it wasn't even called a particle accelerator. It was called a cyclotron, or atom-smasher. If Duste could see Superman unharmed by forces strong enough to smash atoms, then perhaps he'd be convinced that Superman was indeed a supraphysical being. That was one part of my great plot idea. But I was in an extraordinary state. I had also seen something else in that timeless and universal all into which I had plunged as I watched that experiment. I had seen, coming out of that cyclotron, an explosion greater than anyone had ever seen before on earth. It wasn't even a true vision, just a sensation, an idea, an intellectual image of some sort of secondary "big bang." Somehow, without quite knowing why, as Superman stepped out of the cyclotron unharmed and in one piece to confront the startled Professor Duste, he said, "I almost let you see the greatest explosion that ever happened at the same time. But I decided not to. For your own safety. It would have blinded you."

Had I foreseen, during my plunge into the universal, something of what was to come? I don't know. Apparently I did see something I wasn't supposed to see. The Manhattan Project was going full blast at that time. So before that sequence with Professor Duste could appear, the FBI stepped in and censored that segment of the newspaper script on national security grounds.

Nobody ever told me about it. When I finished a continuity, I never sat around and looked for it to appear in the newspapers. So it wasn't until a few years later, after the war, that I happened to see a headline in the *New York Post*: "Superman Had It First." It was the story of how the FBI had censored Superman because the bomb was forecast in the Duste continuity. The FBI had even questioned Jerry Siegel, Superman's originator, thinking he had written that story. Of course Jerry didn't know a thing about it. He still had his name on the strip, but for the past few years I had been writing most of it. Somehow no one got around to telling the FBI investigators that I was the one they should have questioned. Perhaps it was just as well they hadn't. What could I have told them? That I was in a strange clairvoyant state when I wrote that segment? And why hadn't the editors even mentioned it to me until I asked, years later, after coming across that *Post* article?

Even today I don't know. They usually didn't bother telling the writers anything. They were covering up the fact that someone who wasn't Jerry Siegel was writing the script. They were worried about a lawsuit being brought by Siegel and his artist, Joe Shuster, who felt they hadn't been paid enough for their sale of Superman rights. And they were jockeying among themselves for control of various leading characters. Nothing particularly sinister. Just normal interoffice politics. If I had known about it earlier and had asked earlier, they probably would have told me.

This whole congeries of recollections descended on me that night as I sat with Thongden and listened to him tell his story right up to the point where he finally saw the children's fire and they knew he saw it.

He had been watching my face as all my memories and associations came together. Now he said, "You understand?"

I nodded. "First," I said, "I understand that the contact you always maintained with Nelson wasn't telepathy."

"Of course not."

"Until now I assumed it was."

"But now?"

"Now I realize that everything foreshadowed in that BBC experiment was completely correct, that there's a manifest state and an unmanifest state, and if you know how to break through the dimensional walls, you can simply contact anything or create anything through the unmanifest—then there's no need for telepathy. You don't have to go anywhere. You don't have to look for anything. It's there. Beyond the dimensions."

"And how do you get beyond the dimensions?" he asked.

I shrugged. "I suppose it's thought. I suppose thought is real. I don't know. I've stumbled through that gateway a few times. But I don't know how to do it. In fact, a lot of scientists today believe there are as many as eleven different dimensions. I'm only up to managing three—maybe four."

He laughed. "Tell Kay about the unmanifest. Tell her the key is thought. See what she says."

I got up to go. "I'll tell her."

"Tomorrow," he said, "when you come back—we're going to try something different."

Chapter Fifteen

As I told her the whole story, Kay never moved from the couch except once when she went into the kitchen to get a glass of water. Returning, she settled in the exact same spot at the corner of the couch and heard me out without even changing her position. But it was her expression, something in her eyes, that told me I was not making my case as I'd hoped.

"That's all very neat," Kay said when I finally finished. "The manifest and the unmanifest state. But what does it mean?"

"I thought I explained—"

"Wait. What I'm asking is—how does one move back from the unmanifest to the manifest state? There's got to be something else. The ink drop doesn't make that decision. Who turns the crank the other way?"

I sat and thought about that one for a few moments.

Kay went on. "Let's say I die. Or, to use your friend Thongden's language, I become unmanifest. Do I stay dead until someone comes along and uncranks me? Who is that someone? Are we talking about God? In other words, Alvin—what does it all mean for me?"

I looked at her. "I never thought to ask," I admitted.

"He had you too razzle-dazzled," Kay said, pulling that hybrid expression out of a vocabulary that frequently managed to surprise me.

"Maybe," I said, "that'll come up in our next session."

"Anyway," Kay said, getting up from the couch, "I don't think he's a figment of your imagination anymore. I mean—he's real enough. If he weren't, you'd be able to answer my question. If you could invent him, you could invent an answer. But I do think he's conning you for some reason."

"For my money, perhaps?" I joked.

"Look—with all the attention and publicity you've been getting lately over the fact that you were an important Golden Age Superman and Batman writer, who knows what'll come out of the woodwork? Maybe he's just another weird fan. Maybe he just likes keeping you around—on his little string."

"As simple as that," I said, laying the sarcasm on heavily.

"So what you've got to do," she went on as though she hadn't heard me, "is shake him off. Work your way through it all and come back to normal. Or the next thing you know, that Superman phantom he says you've got hanging around you—he'll materialize too, and you'll be talking to him and Thongden. What a threesome."

I realized there was no way to convince her. I also knew that Kay didn't fully believe what she was telling me. She just wasn't sure. So she was playing devil's advocate. It was up to me to prove Thongden's reality—either produce him or find some other way of convincing her. I couldn't really blame her. If our positions had been reversed, I'd probably have reacted the same way.

"I've decided," Kay added, "that you need time to work this out by yourself. When you're between books you get into funny states. Never as bad as this time. But it would probably help if I weren't around for a while to raise questions. You need to do that yourself. So, if you've no objection, I think I'll take a month off and visit my family. We owe Bernette and Naomi a visit."

Bernette was our daughter, who was married to a Calgary businessman. Naomi was our granddaughter from Bernette's first marriage to a Mohawk Indian—a marriage that hadn't worked out. Naomi lived with her mother and stepfather, but, having been born on the Kahnawake Reserve in Quebec, she still kept in contact with her Mohawk roots.

"I'm sure," I said, "that if you're patient a little longer, Thongden will convince you. Show you reality, as he calls it. But—I don't see why you shouldn't go to Calgary. It'll probably be better for both of us if I work this thing out on my own. You're right about that. Besides, Hedy Greene expects me to come up with something for a new book—so getting to Calgary is out for me this year. So really, you should go."

And that settled it comfortably for both of us. That same evening we phoned Bernette. Kay made arrangements to go to Canada while I apologized for the work that kept me from going with her.

Chapter Sixteen

When I returned the next morning, Thongden's living room was back to the way it was when I first saw it. The Tibetan theme with its artifacts had been removed, and Thongden himself was once again wearing a suit. Not a business suit this time but a blazer and a matching pair of slacks. He wore a dark gray shirt, but there was no tie and his collar was open, his feet comfortable in a pair of light brown loafers.

In response to my quizzical look, he held out his big hands as though in acknowledgment of my unuttered question and settled back in his chair. "We're through with the Tibetan saga for now," he explained. "I needed to take you through that, but we're now back to the present." He gave a slight chuckle. "And how did your wife receive your accounting of reality this time?"

I told him in full detail, explaining that Kay was now entertaining the theory that Thongden was basically a fan who just couldn't let go of me. He smiled at my description, crossed one leg over the other, and clasped his hands over his knee.

"She's right, you know. I really am one of your fans," he acknowledged. "By the way, I notice that your Superman image looks a little thin this morning. Kay really got to you, didn't she?" He chuckled for a second time. "Well," he said, before I could reply, "that's to be expected. In fact, things are working out very nicely. She's well on the way to understanding."

"I would have thought just the reverse," I said. "How was I supposed to answer that question of hers—about who turns the crank back?"

"You mustn't load more onto an analogy than it can bear, Mr. Schwartz. Manifest or unmanifest, everything is all in all."

"I don't understand that," I said.

"Not yet. But that's what we're going to delve into next. That's why we're going out today."

"We are?"

He got up, unfolding his long, thin frame until he towered over me. "Nelson once told me that if a man were to acquire a true knowledge of reality in just a few hours, it would probably kill him. It takes time. But Kay will be gone—a month, did you say? That's good. That should be enough time for you both. So be patient."

"Where are we going?" I asked.

"We're going consciousness visiting," he said cryptically as he walked over to the window and peered out. "Perfect weather for it too." He touched my shoulder and directed me to the door. "Come. Let's go."

I followed him outside to the top of the brownstone steps in front of the building. It was a pleasant, brisk, sunny day. Parked at the curb was a taxi, obviously waiting for us. Thongden walked quickly down the steps toward it. I followed, wondering what new revelations were in store for me. My feelings were mixed. I felt elated, as though some exciting adventure awaited me. At the same time I had a vague sense of foreboding. What the devil was Thongden leading me into now? At first my impulse was to dismiss my uneasiness as a normal reaction to venturing deeper into the unknown under the *tulpa*'s direction. But then there flashed into my mind Thongden's own somber comment about Nelson's fearful experience during the night he'd spent watching the *Chod* rites. In telling me about it, Thongden had commented chillingly, "It is not good to deny the reality of the dark powers." I could hear once again the minatory tones in which he had spoken, and glancing up at him now, I seemed to sense another aspect of this strange personality who had burst so unaccountably through the seams of my life. It was as though that facet of Thongden's reality that had so disturbed the monks at Gyo-ling-pa had suddenly revealed itself as lurking behind the benevolence of the *tulpa*'s present aspect. And I recalled, from recent reading in my effort to understand more of what was happening to me, the comments of that respected French scholar and learned Buddhist Alexandra David-Neel about her own experiments in creating a *tulpa*. She apparently succeeded just as effectively as Nelson—a feat she managed to accomplish by visualizing "a monk short and fat, of an innocent and jolly type."

For some time Madame David-Neel kept the *tulpa* around, actually traveling with him until she noticed that his features were gradually changing. In her own words, "The fat chubby-cheeked fellow grew leaner, his face assumed a vaguely mocking, sly malignant look. He became more troublesome and bold. In brief, he escaped my control." She finally decided to dissolve her *tulpa* and managed to succeed, she wrote, only after six months of difficult struggle. "My mind-creature was tenacious of life," she added significantly.[3]

But it was too late to hold back now. So with some uneasiness, I followed Thongden into the cab and settled alongside him. The vehicle started at once, heading east toward Broadway. "The Bronx Zoo," Thongden called through the grate separating us from the driver.

"The Bronx Zoo?" the driver and I repeated in surprised chorus. "That far?" the driver added. "I was on my way to Brooklyn to—"

"I'll pay for your return run," Thongden reassured him. Then, turning to me, "You don't like zoos?"

"Actually—the Bronx Zoo is one of my favorite places. But I don't see how it'll serve your purposes."

"I told you we were going consciousness visiting. There couldn't be a better place."

"You're not going to tell me what you mean?" I asked, looking out the window and noting that the driver was still heading east, probably toward the East River Drive. From there we'd go north to the lower Bronx, then north and east some more. Depending on the traffic, we had possibly a full hour's trip ahead of us. I wondered what Thongden used for money. Did he simply materialize that too? It was a small matter against the background of other questions I had about Thongden, but it manifested as part of my discomfort.

"I am still involved with Nelson's ad hoc group working for the release of Tibet from Chinese oppression," he reminded me, as if in answer to my thoughts. "I am not without roots in the real world." Again he gave the word "real" that unique emphasis that seemed to imply that such reality was only one unit in a much broader category. I nodded, noticing too that he had so far avoided answering my earlier question about what he called consciousness visiting.

Once again, as I thought this, he responded. "Animal consciousness is very complex. Every bit as complex as our own," he said. "But very different. There's no way of explaining it. You have to experience it."

"And how do I do that?"

"When we get there, I will show you." Then, after a pause, he added: "It has something to do with your wife's question about who turns the crank."

I had an unexpected reaction at this point, not just to Thongden's last comment but to the increasing pace of events of the last few days. In many ways my entire world had been turned upside down. My mind, which had not worked so hard for many years, was beginning to feel overwhelmed. Emotionally, too, the level of excitement had been high. For the past couple of decades I had experienced nothing more demanding than locking myself in my room for a few hours at a time and working on a book. While many of my literary colleagues claim that four hours of writing is the equivalent of eight hours of hard labor, there was still no additional outside stress. I had no supervisor, no deadline but my own, no need even to work except my own strong interest in practicing my craft. I was, in fact, largely free of financial pressures since I had enough put aside to ensure a reasonably comfortable existence even if I never wrote another line.

Equally important—my health was good. My heart was sound, and thanks to Kay's insistence that I make regular use of an exercise machine, I was in quite good physical condition for my age. I had long ago freed myself of the joys of smoking and alcohol, and my worst remaining addiction was to caffeine. So all told, I had been enjoying an existence relatively free of necessity, rich in a kind of orderly self-indulgence, and not altogether lacking in what I might call spiritual sensitivity. I was indeed very interested in the significance of my mortality and the meaning and purpose of my life and managed to explore these matters both in my writing and in the material I chose to read. I regarded myself as a believer in what goes by the name of "perennial philosophy"—finding in the sacred works of all the major religions a common orthodoxy. I also found such an orthodoxy in the works of certain great philosophers and literary figures in whom I recognized a similar inspiration. I felt too that much of the new physics tended to rediscover and confirm this same basic orthodoxy. I even realized that such inspiration would from time to time make itself apparent in my own work in such a way that certain things I wrote seemed to come not from my own small ego but quite clearly from a higher source. As far as old age was concerned, it was turning out to be a far more satisfactory state than I had anticipated.

And then Thongden entered my life.

I was admittedly predisposed to certain aspects of the strange new world he revealed to me, perhaps more so because I was not entirely satisfied with the quality of my current work. But I was far from prepared for the kind of strenuous rethinking of my world Thongden brought with him. Beyond this, the undercurrent of fear that went with this reeducation seemed to become especially intensified as we sat in that cab thrusting north and east across two boroughs toward the Bronx Zoo. In reaction, I succumbed to the overwhelming exigencies of thought and experience of the last few days, fell fast asleep, and entered a strange dream.

I was still in the cab. But Thongden had vanished, and sitting beside me was Superman. His cape had draped over him in such a way that the folds seemed somehow frozen into some hard substance. In the new Superman who had recently been appearing on television, the cape was made of ordinary materials stitched together by Ma Kent. And that bothered me because back when I was writing Superman, the cape was made of an indestructible, extraterrestrial material impermeable to bullets, fire, even the tremendous electromagnetic power of a particle accelerator. I had even done a story about Superman's cape—how it was stolen and used as a shield and protective device by the villains who managed to make off with it. So when I looked at the clearly indestructible cape on the Superman who sat beside me in the taxi, I knew my version had been the correct one. I smiled at him. "So—I was right after all. You're the real Superman. The one they've got running around in the TV series and the comics today—they're just impostors with fake capes."

But Superman didn't reply. Indeed, he seemed to be listening to something far off in the distance. Looking out the window, I noticed that we were crossing the 149th Street Bridge connecting Manhattan to the Bronx. Far beyond, down the East River, I could see the 59th Street Bridge to Queens. Something was happening to it. It seemed to be buckling in the center. The suspension towers were dipping down and the whole bridge seemed about to collapse into the river. But Superman had suddenly left the cab and was streaking like a projectile toward the scene of disaster. In another instant he was shoring up the buckled center, straightening the suspension towers, heat-fusing a broken suspension cable—a tiny figure moving so fast I could scarcely follow his movements.

In another moment he had resumed his place alongside me. "Wow!" I exclaimed. "I never thought I'd see anything like—" I broke off my excited words as I noticed that Superman wasn't listening to me at all. He was just sitting motionless beside me, his arms folded as he stared straight ahead. His rescue mission completed, he had simply withdrawn into himself. He had nothing to say to me and no interest in listening to me. Then another voice was saying, "Well—this is where we get off. Did you have a good rest?"

I woke up and saw Thongden standing in the half-open door of the cab, shaking me by the shoulder. "Oh," I said. "I guess I just—"

"—had a good sleep. Good—because we've got a busy day."

I started to get out of the cab. "I had a funny sort of dream," I said. "About Superman."

As I joined him on the asphalt next to the main entrance of the zoo where the cab had deposited us, Thongden appeared to set his gaze on something just over my shoulder. "Yes—I see. He's looking much brighter now than he did this morning."

"The last part of the dream," I said, "didn't make any sense at all. But I guess that's no big surprise."

Thongden gave me a thoughtful look. "Our dreams are us," he said, "but we are not our dreams." He took my arm and led me through the turnstile into the park, suddenly looking his old benign self again.

Chapter Seventeen

*Most disconcerting of all were those experiences
in which the patient's consciousness appeared to
expand beyond the usual boundaries of the ego
and explore what it was like to be living things
and even other objects.*

—Michael Talbot[4]

everal walkways constructed of ten-inch octagonal paving stones
branched off in different directions from a circular area just past
the turnstiles, each leading into a different section of the park.
Small signs were posted at each branching point describing what we
would find along the way.

"Let's try this one," Thongden suggested. The sign revealed that
this was the path to the World of Birds, which included the great aviary as well as separate specimens of the great flightless birds, such as
the ostriches and cassowaries.

Since it was a weekday morning as well as a school day, not many
visitors were about, and for some moments as we proceeded down

the path, there was not another soul in sight. Of those few groups of people we came upon, most turned to stare at Thongden, who, although dressed inconspicuously, could not help attracting attention because of his great height.

"When you are observing other people, it is difficult to see beyond surfaces because you are so used to people. You tend, after adulthood, to see more or less what you already know. That also constitutes an obstacle to consciousness visiting," Thongden was explaining to me as we walked along, glancing casually at some of the exhibits along the way.

"Will you please explain what you mean by consciousness visiting?"

"Perhaps," Thongden went on, "a better term would be 'consciousness transferring.' Perhaps if you practice the technique on animals—the more exotic and unfamiliar, the better—it will come easier."

"Yes—but how—?"

"You start by just looking," he said. "But it is important to prepare the eye to see with portions you don't ordinarily use. People have a tendency to use only a part of their vision, limiting themselves to the visible light spectrum. But the eye's direct connection to the psyche makes it possible to see much more. There are ways of breathing," he continued, "that will renew that forgotten connection."

And then, as we continued walking along, he began to lead me step by step through a complex series of breathing exercises in which short breaths and long breaths alternated, along with various ways of holding one nostril shut while exhaling or inhaling through the other. There were also strong breaths and weak breaths as well as breaths held back until my lungs seemed to be bursting. But apparently the order of these steps was very important, and it was impossible for me to remember them. Besides, instead of achieving anything like the clarity he led me to anticipate, my mind seemed to become cloudy and confused, and I found myself walking alongside him as though in a dream.

I remembered finally peering through the thin bars of a high cage across the surface of a long, dry, grassy plain as a gigantic ostrich started loping swiftly toward me. I seemed to see the lettering on the cage with another part of my eye so that what registered were clumps of word memory: "*Struthio camelus* . . . largest living bird . . . may stand ten feet tall and weigh over 150 pounds . . . speeds up to 70 mph when fleeing predators . . . can use its clawed toes to kick dangerously . . ."

I also seemed to know that this gigantic white-winged, black-feathered creature was a male and even that it had three mates, and as I wondered about that I heard Thongden at the same time exhorting me to set my consciousness into the creature. "Leap," I could hear him saying, and just at that point I saw myself from the other side of the cage, a kind of colorless blob with an odor like paper that seemed to emanate from my clothing. And I had a feeling of floating over the dry grasses as though this too were a kind of flight, a kind of remembered soaring from the dim past that down the eons had shaped itself into this easy bounding, graceful skimming across the living floor of the grass in which was concealed the abundance of succulent berries and small, tasty, wriggling creatures made for finding and swallowing and bringing back to the smaller ones. . . .

I can't say how long it lasted, but after a time I was back watching the creature standing idly nearby, its tiny head turned in my direction and my own human thoughts filled with an awareness of a consciousness for which I had no words because it was so completely unlike mine and yet so—I think I would have to say—selflike. I looked up at Thongden standing beside me. In his eyes I seemed to detect a mixture of amusement and assent, as though I had done well.

"Yes?" he said.

I nodded. My mind was suddenly very clear, possibly clearer than it had ever been. "We aren't just ourselves, are we?" I said, grasping this new thought with a certainty that surprised me.

"Not nearly," Thongden replied with a chuckle. He caught me by the elbow. "Let's go on," he said.

For several minutes as I walked beside him, I had a sense of every-thing around me standing out with greater distinctness, the colors brighter and a shimmering iridescence in the air. I even felt a kind of energy that I hadn't felt in years, as though some husk of years had been broken through. It had to do, somehow, with that sense that my body did not exclusively possess me but rather that I was its possessor, and even the potential possessor of any other bodies that I might choose. It was a most extraordinary feeling, to put it mildly. But it didn't last long. Thongden was now insisting that I return to my breathing exercises.

"You will need them," he explained. "Because there's still the matter of flight. It's very important to explore flight thoroughly— from off the ground."

Of course I didn't have the least idea what he was talking about except that in some way he was alluding to the World of Birds, toward which we were headed.

I could hear the vast chorus of bird sounds well before we rounded a turn in the path and came upon the huge aviary. And then we were there, facing an enormous black birdcage with literally hundreds of small winged creatures flickering freely among the branches of the small trees that furnished it.

The path led us straight inside, and we were suddenly walk-ing among a mass of smaller, multicolored twittering creatures of all shapes and kinds. The air was almost buttery with warmth and humidity. It had been warm outside, but much drier. Most overwhelm-ing was the sense of endless, fluttering motion, the sudden whirring of wings and the soft cries, the shrieks, the croaking notes all blend-ing into a massive cacophony. The breathing exercises, reinforced by Thongden's mesmerizing story of his creation told during long nights in that constantly re-created surreal world he called home, must all have combined to build up in me a kind of heady sensitivity that had, to phrase it appropriately, no edges.

I was again feeling a kind of cloudiness, but it was different this time since I could not seem to distinguish individual birds. Instead I felt swept up into an enormous cloud of feathery bird awareness. I felt weightless and enjoyed a visual acuity that seemed to reveal every inch of ground below me while I vibrated high above it at an intensity in which I was prepared instantly to swoop, dive, rise, wheel, or slide through viscous currents of air. My throat burst with sound, a loving, ululating, pulsing melody, throbbing with a sensation of voluptuous fullness. I felt thoroughly wrapped in that sensation, certain that my call was being heeded and at the same time intensely alert, ready to dart and swerve out of reach of darker shadows and sudden threatening umbras irrupting into the great swarm of vibrating wingtips. Again I don't know how long I remained in that loose and yielding environment. But suddenly I grew gray, somber, and heavy. I felt pulled down to my feet. I felt the weight of my head resting on the bony wings of my shoulders. I was suddenly without motion, all vibration stilled and remote. The world seemed thick and distant and slow. I was myself again, staring at swirling creatures in the aviary and aware of Thongden looking down at me from his great height.

"I would have liked to remain that way," I said almost sadly.

"Every change of consciousness carries its own regrets," the *tulpa* remarked. He had taken my arm again and was leading me back outside.

We walked in silence for a time, down the path away from the aviary. The park was beginning to fill with lunch-hour visitors from the nearby neighborhoods. People were occupying the hitherto empty benches that lined the walkway.

I stopped at one of the benches, indicating to Thongden that I wanted to talk. He assented wordlessly by settling down. I sat beside him, watching groups of people walk past while I marshaled my thoughts. I had been greatly impressed by the experience of flight. From Superman to those birds, I had felt a deep envy. How could humans be superior if we lacked the wondrous free power of flight? I had even experienced and mourned its gradual attrition in the great ostrich.

"You attribute that free feeling to the wrong capacity," Thong-den said, as though once more he had been reading my thoughts.

I shook my head. "It was a wonderful feeling with the birds," I said. "I mean the sheer uninhibited motion—like a dance in four dimensions."

"And Superman? Did he give you the same feeling?"

I shook my head. "Of course I envied it. The way he soared to that collapsing bridge. But it was different. I was on the outside, watching him. He even held me off with his silence. I still don't understand why he ignored me that way."

"He had no choice if he was to do what was necessary."

"That's no explanation," I said. "Is that the best you can do?"

"There's no way I can tell you. You'll have to figure that out for yourself. Maybe the breathing exercises will help."

"Seems mostly like hypnosis to me," I said.

Thongden shook his head. "Here in the West, there's no real understanding of *prajna*. You think breathing is to bring oxygen into your body. Your physiology doesn't get beyond the coarse molecular level. But there's a greater electromagnetic connection with all of life—what you think of as outside yourself. Of course that's impossible. There's no outside, just different positions and attitudes of the self—different magnetic angles. As in certain kinds of flight. Bird flight, such as you've just experienced. But of course that wasn't the flight of a single bird. That was bird flight in general—birdness, you might say. But flight by itself—" He shook his head. "It's really nothing much."

As we talked an old lady sat down on the other end of our bench. I couldn't help noticing her since I was feeling highly sensitized by my recent experiences. She was obviously homeless, dressed in ill-fitting rags and hand-me-downs. She had an old brown coat wrapped around her thick, shapeless frame, the garment spattered with dried remnants of food. There was a great tear in one sleeve. She wore a shabby old wool hat on her head, from under which her white hair strayed in matted, uneven locks that looked stiff and greasy. Her shapeless, once white sneakers were worn over a pair of strangely new bobby socks, which looked clean enough to have been recently acquired.

I kept watching the way her gnarled red hands lay clasped across her lap, from which the handle of a matted straw bag dangled. The sight of her filled me with a mixture of pity, revulsion, and sadness as I wondered what evil conspiracies of time and experience had brought her to this condition.

Of course I had often seen people in her situation. Anyone who visits American cities is confronted by numberless similar unfortunates, especially the mentally ill. But within the intimate purlieu of our bench, this woman did not seem to be among those. In fact, from her expression I could detect only a quiet resignation and what struck me as a poignant awareness of herself.

In all, it was a fleeting impression, the product of a glance in which I detected a few familiar signs and filled in the rest. It was the way most of us tend to perceive things most of the time. And then Thongden was quietly urging me to get on with my breathing again.

This time he presented me with a new set of instructions, as though, using the same old notes, he had constructed an entirely new musical score. The rhythms were different, the sustained inhalations and exhalations were longer, and the alternations between nostrils were also unlike his previous instructions. By now I managed to listen to him and follow his instructions while part of my mind gradually separated itself, following my eyes, which traveled now from the old woman to that tear on her coat sleeve, onto which I saw a large fly settle, its antennae working swiftly in a lowered position, the two separate strands winding around each other and then unwinding in some tremendous agony of impatience and terror. Above these feelings was a kind of erratic humming that suddenly grew to a roar, and I was looking down at the great expanse of sleeve, which swooped up and away at me as I felt the rising panic of shapes breaking out on all sides so that suddenly I went skittering off against the side of a tree, settling into a deep crevasse in the bark like a draft of sweetness and stickiness coupled with the still pursuing menace. And instantly I was off again, drawn by the stickiness of the coat sleeve, diving wildly toward the odorous morsel under the loose strand above the great gaping hole, antennae outstretched while erratically dodging, watching, careening from the buzz and swish of the down-plunging, still pursuing menace.

Flight once more, harsh, erratic, buzzing desperately, longing to find rest and a secure place where the fleeing could end, where the looseness and emptiness of flashing from one point to another would release me and I could luxuriate in a long stillness. . . .

"—so, as you might note, flight itself is merely the shortest distance between two restful points," I heard Thongden saying. "Not in itself an attribute to be envied."

I was back on the bench, but the familiar cloudy feeling was not present. And I seemed to be hearing Thongden from a distance. He was talking to me, *and I was watching him do it.*

I could see myself, but not clearly. My mind was clear, but my vision was blurred. I raised my hand and adjusted the glasses dangling too low on my nose. They were hand-me-downs, store magnifiers that had been given to me at the East Bronx Community Foodbank. By holding them out a little and twisting the left side forward, I could read fairly clearly. Now, adjusting the glasses, I could see the two of them as they sat on the bench beside me—the little old man with the quick hands and lively face and the tall Chinaman. The little old man had been watching me, and I could see I made him uncomfortable. I felt like touching him and telling him it was all right. I wondered if he'd believe me if I told him I was having such fun today. The park was so full of new people, even people like himself and his friend, who was trying to make him blow through his nose in a funny way as though he needed to clear an obstruction. Only I don't think it was a physical thing. His mind was so sensitive to hurt. I knew he was feeling bad about me. I can always tell. How could I reassure him? How would he react if I said to him, "There now—you don't have to take on so about me. I never felt freer in my life." When you don't even have yourself to worry about, when it doesn't matter if you're not always warm during the cold spells, and not always getting enough to eat and not liking the nights in the shelter, and the arthritis pains in the knees and neck and fingers—when you discover that it's not *you* who has the problem—so the real you can sit back and take it as it comes—how can I tell him he's worrying about the wrong thing? Oh—and here are my pigeons. They can tell when I've got a few extra crumbs for them in my bag. I don't have to explain anything to them.

One gnarled old hand unclasped itself from the bag handle while it reached inside and came up with some crumbs of stale bread. One of the pigeons was already on the old lady's lap, and I turned my head away, realizing suddenly where I'd been and that I was back now, looking at Thongden with that fine pair of eyes that only needed to depend on glasses when reading or driving at night.

"I just got my comeuppance," I said to him, smiling suddenly, feeling delighted with the old lady and, by a kind of magical induction, with myself. "Do you know, I feel hungry. I guess that fact wouldn't concern a *tulpa* who functions only on osmosis."

Thongden offered a halfhearted shrug. "Sometimes, in good company, I enjoy the ceremony of eating," he said. "Shall we find some place? I think there was a restaurant sign back along the path. It pointed ahead. Probably not far."

I got up and he joined me. As we started walking, I said, "When I get into another consciousness like that and I'm suddenly not me anymore—not Alvin Schwartz, I mean. Then who the hell am I? I mean, who's the one that keeps going back and forth?"

"Ah," Thongden said with a smile. "Now you're asking the right question." I knew that was as much as he was going to tell me for the time being.

We didn't get to the restaurant as soon as I'd hoped. For one thing, we found ourselves circling back to where the paths first forked. Then we took an altogether different path, and this time we found ourselves circling through forty acres of what was known as the Wild Asia Exhibit, whose specially prepared landscapes were the domain of elephants, great cats, camels, primates, and even a number of species of Asian bears. For some reason Thongden decided then and there that we should go on an elephant ride, joining an assortment of children and young people. We sat on a multiseated saddle with two sides hanging over the great creature's flanks as he went shambling slowly around a well-worn track with the skewed rocking motions of a ship with a damaged rudder. And Thongden didn't stop there, urging me into further breathing exercises so that from being the rider, I became the ride, the old elephant himself, and was somewhat surprised to find, as in the case of the old lady, a very contented creature.

There were several more of these consciousness transfers as we went along. I found myself in the mind of an angry, tormented, and jealous gorilla who had to watch helplessly as another larger gorilla made out with the only available female, and I was amazed to discover how much the animal's feelings resembled the human, although it seemed to me there was better control and more acceptance, not resignation, on the part of the rejected primate.

There were more instances, and in each case my awareness of self became more tenuous, more questioning. At last, when the park restaurant was in sight, I asked Thongden once more what it meant when I used the word "I" if I could use it with equal significance in whatever consciousness he had me enter.

"An 'I' comes into being," he said, "whenever you choose to limit yourself." He spoke reluctantly, out of politeness because I had kept pressing the question.

"And who's the 'I' that chooses to do that?" I asked. We were already inside the restaurant and following a bustling hostess dressed in the blue and yellow colors that seemed to be the park's chromatic theme. "And why choose limits anyway?"

"Two different questions," Thongden said, settling at the small table for two the hostess selected for us somewhere in the middle aisle. "I'll answer the second one first by reminding you that the answer is already known to you. Superman—he chooses limits. Why does he become Clark Kent?"

I smiled. "So no one should know who he really is?" I said, repeating my son's long-ago comment to Dr. Mittelman.

"You know better," Thongden said, "You asked me twice this morning why your Superman remains so silent after his rescues. Don't you understand this yet?"

"No," I said, scanning the menu while the waitress arrived and hovered over us.

"In some ways he's the most difficult of all. You haven't gotten into his consciousness yet, as you have all the others. In fact, getting into—"

"Are you gentlemen ready to order?" the waitress asked.

"Oh," I said. "This Bronx doubleburger with cheese and french fries. That's for me—a total cholesterol plunge. Just this once, to celebrate."

The waitress looked at Thongden. "The mixed salad," he said.

"Drinks?"

"Coke," I said.

"Coke," Thongden echoed. As the waitress started away, he picked up his thought once more. "Getting into the consciousness of a *tulpa* is probably the most difficult of all because basically the *tulpa* exists because of an effort at separation. You're trying to externalize yourself. It's like looking into a mirror, actually, in order to see yourself, when really you're one step further away. You have to look inside, not outside."

"You mean I ought to give up on Superman? Thongden, I never even knew I was creating him until you told me about it."

"And you'll have to finish doing that. And then you'll have to try getting inside your own created image."

"But—why?"

"Then you'll have the answer to the question you just asked. Why is Superman so silent after one of his rescues?"

"Are you going to help me do it?" I asked.

Thongden nodded. "That's what we've been leading up to all along. But there's no way of doing it directly."

And with that further cryptic remark, our food arrived. It was already late afternoon, and I wolfed my hamburger without saying another word, hardly even noticing as Thongden picked quietly and with little interest at his salad.

At the time I didn't particularly notice I was doing it. But every few seconds I'd lift my eyes and do a circuit of the room and stop at a particular table where a young woman of perhaps twenty was also eating, working her way through a salad like Thongden. Glancing at pretty women was not something I had lost the habit of. I don't actually remember a time when I didn't do it, no matter what my age. In fact, it was so habitual that I wasn't always aware of it. Kay noticed it sometimes, and she'd tease me, but it didn't bother her. I didn't leer. I didn't ogle. I didn't even try to flirt. All I did was notice. If there was a pretty woman anywhere within eyeshot, I noticed. It was a reflex that, I assumed, went along with being a male of the species, and I never gave it a second thought. Nor apparently did Kay.

So there I was, and my eyes must have traveled at least a dozen times to that pretty woman about three tables away from ours, just near the window where the light fell on her face. I kept talking with Thongden when I wasn't busy gulping my food—and furtively directing my eyes toward that table. At first it was rather automatic. But by now I had become uncomfortably aware that I was doing it, and wondered why. So I began to take more notice.

She was rather small, with short dark hair pushed back behind her ears and dark eyes and quick, graceful movements of the hands.

She wore an informal long shirred skirt and white blouse and looked a little old-fashioned in that setting. I also noticed her long earlobes and that she wore large dangling turquoise earrings—apparently true Navajo artifacts. I'm quite farsighted and at the proper distance, as I was now, few details escaped me.

Did I say she was pretty? Not quite the right word. I tried to express it to myself to account for the fact that I kept getting drawn to her with a magnetism well beyond the attractors of any normal male reflex. Looking at her seemed to evoke powerful associations—the outlines of hazily recalled events, intimations of walking and hand-holding and sharing confidences, heads held together and touching, along with a familiar feminine scent accompanied by a background redolence of chalk and schoolrooms. A real memory? Or just a daydream? Was there something familiar about her, then? I couldn't say exactly. Not while I was just observing her from the security of distance and anonymity. And then, unexpectedly, it all changed. She must have felt me watching her because she looked across and our eyes met. For some surprising moments, they held. An expression of surprise flitted across her features. I saw thin furrows appear in her forehead. She looked away and looked back again, this time openly frowning. Was she trying to recognize me too? Had I known her once long ago? The difference in our ages denied the possibility.

But something about the curve of her jaw to the lovely dip of her chin—the way her hand lifted to brush back an errant lock of hair—and suddenly I was blushing. I could feel the familiar flush suffusing my cheeks just as it had long ago during my high school years when a certain very important former steady who had only too recently cast me off would walk in with some message or other for my teacher. As I sat in my second-row seat in Latin class, her abrupt, unanticipated appearance would force a blush to spread wildly across my cheeks. It wasn't long before my observant class-mates began to connect the manifestation with her arrival, and I quickly became the butt of their jokes. This was the same blush, but now I had a full beard and it remained invisible. But—what was happening? Had the young lady recognized me? And why did I slip into that agonized, melancholy mode of the rejected lover? I had been many things that day, explored many consciousnesses, but as I sat there in wonder I was fully aware of the fact that I was a balding, white-haired, round-shouldered old man who could easily be her grandfather. I glanced at Thongden, but he appeared not to notice as, head down, he continued to pick at his food.

I decided to keep my own head down too. This was not something I wanted to get drawn into. And yet it was strange. Why *did* she seem so familiar to me? And why that intimation of recognition from *her*?

But I resisted the impulse to glance toward her table again. Preoccupied with my own immediate affairs, I made the casual gesture of brushing away a fly that was hovering too close to my plate. I should mention that the restaurant was really a kind of outdoor affair. The windows were not closed off from the park itself. They were elongated panels that could be closed in the event of bad weather but were presently wide open to the outside. Which, of course, invited the flies as well. I thought of that as, for a second time, my hand was poised to brush away the same fly that now had settled on the edge of my plate.

Just then, an errant thought entered my mind. "What if—?" I stopped, not allowing the thought to shape itself into so many words. But the thought was there, fully formed, nonetheless. I drew my hand back and stared at the fly, watching those antennae corkscrewing together in an investigatory manner over something invisible on the edge of my plate. Because I had done this before, I realized I knew how to do it again. It needed only some sort of internal push. Then I sensed that Thongden was watching me. I looked up. His fork was poised motionless about three inches from his mouth. His eyes rested on me with a new speculative expression.

"What?" I said.

"Even a fly—" he began, then seemed to hesitate.

"You think I shouldn't—" I began, knowing he had guessed my thoughts.

"It is possible, even with a fly. There's even a kind of identity in, say, a puddle of water left over by the rain."

I didn't understand what he was getting at, and my expression must have shown it. He proceeded to explain further. "To transfer consciousness is not a great feat. It does not reveal very much. But to transfer consciousness while staying in control with your own consciousness—that puts you squarely on the Path without Form."

"Explain," I said, sensing that somehow we had come to the real point of the day's outing.

Thongden settled back in his seat, laying down his fork. "Normally you see things from the outside. Seen that way, your world is made up of objects. Objects are fixed both in space and in time. They share what is called in Sanskrit *nama-rupa,* name and form. From this arises the sense of separation, of desire, and the illusion of mortality. Things fixed in space and time have only so much space and so much time. They exist by virtue of limitation."

I sat there thinking that at one time or another I had heard or read all this before. But what did it mean in a practical way? I was about to find out.

"Did I not tell you earlier that there's no outside, just different positions and attitudes of the self—different magnetic angles?" Without waiting for my reply, he asked, "Mr. Schwartz, have you ever wondered why one cannot see from the *inside*? Is there a law that keeps you bound to the outside—to the external? Is there a law that says you are fixed in just one moment of time, at one moment of your age, at one place only? Your purpose in being here today is to abandon that prejudice by entering the Path without Form."

"And how will I do that?"

"You have already started on it."

"In what way?"

"You don't see? That girl you've been watching. Do you imagine for a moment that you could recognize her in your ordinary objective world?"

"You mean—" I glanced once more toward the woman at the window table. She looked very objective to me. But somehow, that feeling of familiarity—was that what Thongden meant?

The fly was buzzing over my plate again. I was about to brush it off once more when I paused, caught Thongden's eye, and saw him nod.

"Again—that fly," he said.

"Yes—" I admitted sheepishly.

"But how would fly consciousness serve your human curiosity? All it would investigate of that girl would be of interest only to a fly."

"That occurred to me."

"Then why not take your Alvin self along too?"

"I don't understand."

"On the Path without Form you don't have to carry your prejudices with you."

"You mean I could?"

"You need only permit yourself to be fully *inside*."

I did not resist. Thongden had brought me to a state where now I had only to let go. Finally I believed it. I let myself drop away.

The material on the plate was now big enough to see. It was a sugary dropping—a bit of dried hemoglobin from the hamburger, rising like a flat-topped mountain splitting the gigantic roll on my plate. I snatched it up and then felt that menacing vibratory buzzing and pressure of frenzied flight and tore into the air, skittering about in wide, loose circles as I moved toward the window and that table I had earlier been avoiding and which I knew I was not avoiding now. I felt all the terror and the driven desperation of before, but I also felt apart from it, as though this time I was not just that fly but had

another kind of awareness, as though in assuming the fly consciousness I had not completely let go of my own. Did I say "my own"?
I'm not really sure *what* was my own at that moment. Because even
as I was driven by that disordered and paranoid fly consciousness,
my *other* consciousness was somehow directing, encouraging, steering the fly in a way that directed its flight toward the woman at
the table, although she was now nothing more than an uprushing
pyramidal mass of colors and textures and mysterious emanations.
I landed on her shoulder. I think it must have been her shoulder,
because one of those enormous turquoise shapes—the earrings I had
noted earlier—hung like a gigantic rugged black and blue boulder
just over the point where I landed on the branchlike filament of
her shirt. So it had to be the shoulder. And out of that sense of
expanded awareness, the Alvin awareness exponentially increased
as it absorbed the fly awareness—I realized that what I called "I"
had grown even more complex. One did not merge into the other,
as I realized, but rather was linked by awareness itself, something
vast and undifferentiated. Without judgment or desire, it noted that
olfactory presence of hers. That was all. The skittering fly movement
resumed its wide circling back once more to my plate and left me
looking down at it, remembering the unique perfume she wore with
its poignant association of lost adolescence.

Thongden was speaking now, and I managed to raise my eyes
from my plate. He was saying something about my having been taking minute steps all day along the Path without Form.

"Really?" I said, barely hearing him and certainly not understanding him.

"Let me," he persisted quietly, "disentangle you a little. You
know, for example, about the nature of light?"

Was he trying to distract me or tell me something? Or warn me?
There was something disconcerting about his expression. I sensed
disapproval along with an ill-concealed anger. My earlier foreboding
had returned. "If you mean that it is sometimes like a particle and

sometimes like a wave—I suppose yes. It's never accurate to say it's either one or the other. But why?"

"So when you encounter more than one 'I'—you can understand that one is no more true than another. Every 'I' is real. But not at the same time."

I turned my head away and glanced toward that other table. The young woman was gone. I felt such a stab of panic, I stood up.

"The Path without Form," Thongden was saying. "It is possible for you to explore it much more than you have. But it is dangerous. Very dangerous. Still—if you persist, you must put more power into your thoughts."

I was already moving away from the table as he spoke. I didn't pay too much attention to his words, but they left their imprint. As I hurried out of the restaurant onto the walkway that had brought us here, I heard the words repeating themselves in my head. Then I looked down the path and there she was, walking slowly, her sling purse resting over one shoulder while one hand rested against its dangling side. She had a longish stride for a small person. She walked with assurance, her toes pointed directly ahead. I could stand there and keep her in sight along that straight portion of the path for some time. I was positioned now less than three feet from the table where she'd been sitting. Her vacated chair was still pulled back. And suddenly I wanted to do something crazy. It was that olfactory aura of hers that drew me. But also—something else—another kind of memory. What was it? Why was I specifically drawn to her chair?

It came to me almost at once—something I had read years ago in a Faulkner novel, *The Hamlet*. The sexy schoolgirl, Eula Varner, tempting the protagonist to press his cheek to her just-vacated school bench. Hardly a spontaneous feeling on my part. An old literary image out of a book I had read decades ago.

And then it occurred to me that our feelings mostly get acted out in ways previously learned. We each of us maintain a stock of preexistent patterns we seize upon when powerful emotions need expression. And that's where the sense of separation begins.

Having found the pattern for my crazy impulse, I resisted it. I was on a formless path now. But I still couldn't understand the powerful emotion that evoked the impulse. What had gotten hold of me? Who was this mysterious, lovely, and terribly familiar young woman?

Ignoring Thongden, I set off down the path after her.

Chapter Eighteen

followed but kept a safe distance between us. Somehow I had to find a way of approaching her. But then what? The feelings she had roused in me were shareable only between contemporaries. I had seen that flicker of recognition in her eyes and then seen it fade as though my age had suddenly annulled whatever connection she might have imagined from a quick glance. Perhaps a familiar gesture, some trace of a vanished group of features briefly obtruding from my worn timescape of a face, had briefly caught her attention and then as quickly faded as she took in the details.

So far this had been the strangest day of my life, exceeding even the day of my first meeting with Thongden. I had been guided, shaped, *prajna*-formed, and distributed into a multitude of consciousnesses. I had experienced myself as an ostrich, a flock of exotic birds, an old woman, a fly, and a variety of large mammals. I had learned that the thing I thought of as "I" had an incredible plasticity that allowed some fundamental selfness to shift through all these changes without getting lost in any of them even while fully immersed in them. Even at this moment, in the carapace of an old man, I was shadowing this mysterious young woman who in some way shared a memory link with me that I needed to reexperience. But who really was doing the shadowing? Alvin, the old man? Clearly not. There was another, younger Alvin, her actual contemporary, somehow still real, still present, through whom I could present myself to her. Hadn't Thongden said that on this "path" one was not bound to any particular time? How did he mean that?

I was thinking in such wild terms because I had already been preconditioned. I believed I was beginning to see my way more clearly along what Thongden had just called "the Path without Form." He had said, with some reluctance, I felt, that I needed to put more power into my thoughts. And then, as I continued to follow my dream lady, as I had already begun to think of her, I saw her turn unexpectedly off our path and onto another that intersected it some fifty yards ahead. Losing sight of her in that moment, I felt a spasm of profound loss. It must have shown on my face because a couple coming toward me turned to look at me as they came alongside, as though my sudden grimace had startled them.

And with this came a surge of something like energy, but it was really a burst of thought, a kind of breaking loose of the imagination. It wasn't an altogether unfamiliar feeling. I'd experienced something like it from time to time at special moments while working on a book, when unexpectedly words, ideas, directions broke loose in a great clump and the work seemed to leap ahead on its own. But I'd never felt it quite like this—*as though I had suddenly become pure imagination*. It was the abrupt sense of loss that precipitated it, I'm sure. But it began with the sudden conviction that consciousness shifting was, as Thongden had said, no more limited to any particular time than it was to any particular "I."

I remembered, in the same "bundle" of imagination, Thongden's remark about his being able to see all those images of other important personalities in my life that were thronged about me along with my personal Superman phantasm, the images that, he said, would brighten at the moment of my death. So, in a sense, I realized, in some manner, all of that past, all of my significant yesterdays, was somehow still with me.

Here, in this state that was like pure imagination, could I not shift in time just as I had in place? Could I not shift into my own youthful yesterday out of which that dream lady had somehow emerged?

The thought translated itself in a surprising way, not at all as I'd expected or dared to hope. I didn't leap into some wondrous youthful self. I just kept walking, but much faster than before, toward the point where she'd vanished down that intersecting path. And then there were two joggers coming up behind me, both in track suits—a couple maybe in their thirties. I didn't want to let them pass me. Besides, it was taking me too long to reach that intersection where she'd turned off. I started to run. I could feel the smoothness and tensility of my leg muscles as I fell easily into long runner's strides. And then I was really going full tilt, faster than I had in years. I could feel my toes springing off the ground, my heels not even touching. I was way ahead of the joggers, and I had to grab a post as I swung around the intersection. I looked far ahead down the path. She was nowhere in sight. But there was a rise in the path that crested about a hundred yards ahead. Since there was no place to turn off, I assumed she must have gotten to the other side of the rise. I burst into a full dash, enjoying the surge of power that lifted my legs and extended my stride. I was running the way I had on the high school track team. I felt a strong rush of wonder and excitement. I felt the whole world going out of focus, then dimming. For nanoseconds, the universe itself seemed to vanish. It was like a scene shift in a theater, accomplished solely with light. In an instant it all came back, but clearer, brighter, empty of the dullness and accretions of time. And as I crested the rise, I saw her. She was walking slowly now, about fifty feet ahead of me.

I slowed down. To my surprise I was breathing easily. But I could feel beads of sweat on my forehead. I raised a hand to brush the moisture away. With a shock, I felt the smooth, bland shape of my forehead. I brushed my fingertips across the same spot a second time. No—I hadn't been mistaken. The familiar deep furrows had somehow smoothed out. I glanced down at my hand as it came away from my forehead. The knuckles had retreated and the veinous protuberances had shrunk back into fine blue lines.

I didn't have to go through the rest of it to know that I had somehow broken through. I knew it, and I was convinced that I'd also crossed some line that marked the outpost of sanity. I ran my hands over my face. There was no beard now. But I could feel the day's slight accumulation of stubble.

And then fear came cascading through. I was out of control. Lost in limitless possibility, as though what was "I" suddenly had no shape, no place, no proper time of its own. It was like being scattered, dispersed—an undefined force drifting aimlessly across—what? I kept trying to remind myself that this was only an aftereffect of all those complex breathing exercises. It was temporary, I told myself. In another moment I would be myself again. All I had to do was hold on, avoid panic. I took a long, deep breath. And then, suddenly, she turned and looked straight at me.

I began slowly running again, partly out of confusion, partly out of fear. As I was pacing past her, she gave me a puzzled smile. I returned a stiff nod but continued on, too confused to let the situation develop any further in spite of all my earlier wishes. I needed time to adjust, to decide what was happening to me. I didn't want to be trapped into the feeling for her into which I was being swept. Because if by some miraculous extension of Thongden's consciousness transfer technique I had indeed become youthful, how long would I remain in that state? And where would it lead? And finally, what about Kay? She would suddenly have become old enough to be my grandmother. And what would I be to my own children?

But of course I knew this had to be a temporary state. Otherwise all barriers were down. With every possibility open, there were really no possibilities at all. Only confusion and dissociation. In gathering concern I moved on, looking for another intersection from which I could circle back to Thongden, voice my regret about not having heeded his warning, and then get his help without having to pass my dream lady again. I feared another meeting of our eyes.

I slowed to a walk, looking past the carefully tended shrubbery at the margins of the path for another opening. What happened next was so unexpected that I could only react. There was no thought, no caution, no prejudgment. I simply reacted. Because there she was, right behind me and running, purposely pursuing me.

"Why did you do that?" she said. Her voice was a kind of liquefied honey with an odd burr in it that bordered, like so many things about her, on the edge of the familiar.

"Me—you mean me?"

"I don't see anyone else running away from me," she remarked, turning her head back and forth in a kind of mock search of the path.

"This—" I said, trying to find the thought and shape it into words that made sense, "—has never happened to me before."

She stood there watching me, her head tilted slightly to one side. "Well—why should it have?"

"Because," I began, then broke off and tried a new tack. "You know about this? About what's happening?"

Again our eyes met and words simply fell away. We hung on each other's gaze for several long seconds. I felt my heartbeat ripple down through my chest and set up a pounding through my whole body.

"No," she said finally. "Not this." There was something very direct about her. She reached out her hand and took mine. Her touch was cool and firm. "Let's just walk for a while," she said.

We were on a side path that brought us to a different group of mammals—members of the dog family, or, as the sign indicated, *Canidae*. Just beyond the fence at the left side of the path was a kind of rocky landscape rising in low, flat terraces and covered by soil on which a kind of prairie grass was growing. Within each rocky ledge, of which there appeared to be three levels, were openings like miniature caves.

She stopped at this point, releasing my hand as she pointed toward the carefully structured exhibit. "The fox dens," she said, pointing toward the ledges.

"Was this where you were headed?" I asked, nonplussed.

"I stop by every afternoon after work. Foxes fascinate me."

"Do they?" I said, wondering suddenly whether my infatuation wasn't turning out to be a kind of self-created emotional fraud. "Why foxes?"

She turned to face me, presenting me with a smile that overwhelmed my sudden doubts. "It does sound a little kooky, doesn't it? But you know—foxes are solitary creatures. Because they hunt small prey. Usually enough just to feed one. So they don't hunt in packs. That solitariness is very special in a mammal. It makes for a kind of wiliness and independence. And—yes—a kind of restless cleverness." She laughed suddenly. "Foxy—you know?"

"And why does all this interest you?" As I spoke, a small red fox suddenly appeared in one of the rocky openings—just emerging from its den as it stopped and looked warily in our direction as we stood some twenty yards away.

She shrugged. "I'm a very separate person myself. Oh—and part Indian. Does that explain it?"

"You do look a bit Indian. But—is that it?"

I thought of my Indian granddaughter, but there was no resemblance, no possible connection.

She shook her head. "Not exactly." She rested one small hand on my wrist. "Call it a kind of confidence. A personal outreach—from me to you. Showing you my foxes like this. You see?"

She was beginning to make just a bit more sense in a subtle way. "But why such solitariness? I mean you, not the foxes."

She shrugged. "It's how I am." She turned suddenly to the watching fox and began making a kind of quick chittering sound with her lips and tongue. The small animal's ears perked up. And then it ran toward her. She reached her hand through the fence. The fox nipped carefully at the hand, then licked at the outstretched fingers. *"Ah—Reynard—je suis un peu tard. Tu m'attends longtemps?"*

"You didn't learn French on your Indian side," I said.

"No," she said, standing again. "The Acadian side. You know about Acadians?"

"I know that two hundred years ago the British drove them from their northern homes and they scattered all the way down the East Coast, with a lot of them winding up in New Orleans."

"My own family never left the Maritimes. My grandparents spoke French and Micmac. I went to school in English, but we spoke French at home."

"And Micmac?"

"Even the Indians hardly speak Micmac anymore."

"You're from New Brunswick?" So was Kay, but that didn't explain anything. Another coincidence.

She nodded. "Tracadie." It was a village that jutted into the Atlantic from the mouth of the St. Lawrence in northern New Brunswick. Again—no connection. Kay was from Bathurst, thirty miles west of Tracadie.

"I'm from New York."

"The Bronx?"

I shook my head. "No—Manhattan." And then I had the strange feeling that she was going to ask me when I was born. I fell silent and waited for her question. Again our eyes met, and with the meeting came that feeling of quiet, inexplicable familiarity and closeness. But she didn't ask. She took my hand.

"Now we are getting to know one another again," she said.

That single word—"again"—took me by surprise. "Then you remember—?"

I never finished my sentence. She pressed a couple of fingers to my lips to stop me. "There's something we have to relearn," she said. "It will come if we give it time."

I was astonished. So it was happening to her too. She felt the familiarity but couldn't explain it. The realization made me less cautious. I wanted to open up that mystery at once. I started with another question. "You said you come here in the afternoons—after work?"

She nodded.

"What kind of work?"

I felt her fingers reach for mine and close tightly around them. "It is a very nice feeling when I hold your hand like this," she said.

"Yes," I said, thinking that it was like reexperiencing the wonders of first love. "But you didn't answer my question."

We walked along in silence, still holding hands. Finally she said, "It is too soon."

I was about to press her further on that, but we had come to another turn in the path. The shrubbery had grown quite high here and was bursting into full summer leaf, so it would have been impossible to see around the turn. We almost ran into Thongden, who was coming down the path from the opposite direction.

"Ah—" he said. "There you are." He offered a slight bow of greeting to my companion.

"Ah—" I repeated a similar drawn-out aspirate to hide my discomfort. I had actually forgotten that I'd left him in the restaurant. I pointed to my companion. "This is—" And again I was at a loss. I hadn't yet learned her name.

"Louise," she said, holding out her hand.

Thongden took it, stooped, and touched his lips to the back of her extended fingers. They were both suddenly being very continental, I thought with poorly concealed irritation. Why had he chosen to come after me now?

"Mr. Thongden," he said, introducing himself to her. "I was looking for my friend here," he added, indicating me with an upsweep of the hand. "He saw you in the restaurant and left our table so fast—"

"I had no idea you minded," I said acidly.

"True—you had no idea of anything except this young lady," he said, smiling. He repeated her name: "Louise."

"I'm so glad he did," she replied, looking fondly in my direction. "It's been so long—" And she broke off, a confused expression shadowing her features for an instant, before she added, "I mean—since we last saw each other." There was a rising inflection in her voice as though the statement were really a question directed at me.

"Yes," I said lamely. "So long since the last time."

"But," Louise said, glancing down at the watch on her left wrist, "it's late."

I noticed there were large oblong turquoise stones set into the band, matching the turquoise earrings.

"I have to go," she said. "It's been a strangely exciting day."

"You can't go," I protested in alarm.

"I'll be here again tomorrow afternoon," she promised.

"Will you meet me?"

"Of course. At the foxes." And she turned and started off down the path in the same direction we'd been walking.

I could feel Thongden watching me watching her as she slowly disappeared from view. For some reason, without turning to face him directly, I sensed something truly baleful in his look. And this time I knew I was not imagining it.

Chapter Nineteen

We didn't talk much in the cab on the way back to Thongden's place. And I didn't fall asleep either. I was still in a restless, excitable state and kept looking out the cab window, not seeing anything in particular but reliving the highlights of what had been a most memorable day. Without looking at him, I could sense Thongden gazing at me in some unfathomable way as he sat back in the shadows of the cab. I had again become extremely uncomfortable in his presence. I was even convinced that there had been a subtle change in his appearance—that his face had become leaner and narrower. And there was a glint of something in his eyes that intimated his nonhuman origin.

"How does it feel to be young again?" he asked, as it seemed to me almost too blandly. It was the only bit of conversation he initiated during that return ride.

"I don't know," I said, "There's a lot I don't understand." Before leaving the zoo, I had spent some twenty minutes examining myself in the washroom mirror. I looked as though I were over fifty years younger. Oddly enough, even though I was thinner the clothes I wore had somehow accommodated themselves to my leaner frame. Thongden waited patiently for me, watching me go through this self-examination without any comment or change of that fixed expression he'd worn since we had separated from Louise. Then, when I'd had enough of myself, we headed out and found the cab that was now taking us back to Manhattan.

I was hoping he might begin to explain a few things, such as how I could have gone back in time that way without anything on the outside being any different. I kept thinking of the dot floating on the glycerine in the cylinder with the crank. Maybe it was because the dot itself was divisible into smaller and smaller dots even in the manifest state—a little like particle physics, in which researchers kept discovering smaller and smaller particles while at the same time also discovering that particles really didn't exist at all except as mathematical concepts or the points of manifestation of a single wave along a continuum. But what then was it that got cranked into the glycerine? If the dot was just an idea—and so on . . . My thoughts helplessly roamed through impossible thickets until I began to suspect that anything was possible and nothing and everything was real. And that the Path without Form was, indeed, utterly formless.

By the time we got back to Thongden's brownstone, I was in a very confused state. It was nearly seven o'clock when we arrived. I hadn't brought my car, and I had missed the last commuter train home. At the same time, I was ravenously hungry.

If your mind gets to be too much for you, rely on your stomach, I decided. I sent out for another Reuben sandwich. It seemed to be the right kind of solid food to balance crashing at Thongden's for another night. Besides, I knew we had a lot to talk about. By the time we settled down and I'd had my meal, which Thongden regarded as rather barbaric—as though the combination of sauerkraut and corned beef burned into two hunks of rye bread were the product of a degenerate civilization—I was full of talk and ready with dozens of questions. By now, too, I was feeling almost comfortable again with the *tulpa*. Only an iota of my earlier foreboding remained, like a bad lurking headache.

But before I even got around to asking my first question, he confounded me by bringing up another subject altogether. He sat there on the floor in the lotus position, having changed from his street clothes into a loose gold brocaded robe with kimono sleeves, and announced, "Of course it all has to do more with Superman than with your turquoise lady."

"How did you know to call her that?" I commented, seizing on the less important part of his statement.

"You send out such strong signals," he said, smiling. "But I think you really want to know about Superman."

"I'm so glad you can save me the trouble of asking," I responded tartly.

"On the Path without Form, it is difficult to know how things will turn out. You understand why?" And without waiting for me to reply, he went on, "Because it is like a left hand and a right hand in empty space. On the Path without Form, there is no third element, no reference point to tell you which is right and which is left. So everything is probability."

"Probability of what?" I said, more confused than ever.

"That you will go left when the pass is to the right." He had taken on a very grave expression as he continued. There was even a small frown shaping itself on his broad, otherwise smooth forehead. "These are the deciding moments for every one of us. From time to time in life, people confront such moments. There are many things they try to do in these moments. But there is only one thing to do. It was such a moment as Rimpoche Nelson confronted when he found me and faced the requirement to dissolve me."

"And he did nothing," I said.

"Precisely. At such a time, one must do nothing. The best action is—nonaction."

"I understand less and less," I said. "First you tell me it has more to do with Superman—and then you tell me to do nothing. Exactly what *are* you telling me?"

"The answer to your question about Superman's strange silence."

"I still don't understand."

"Be patient. On the Path without Form you can only assume that the universe is running as it should. You cannot interfere. To avoid unforeseen consequences, you must not act. Everything will come together. Superman will play his part. And you will understand his silence. But only if you learn the most important lesson of all—nonaction. Noninterference."

I considered his words, trying to find a glimmer of clarity in them. But all I heard was warning—and under that a kind of obscure menace. "Does that mean," I asked, "that I should not meet Louise tomorrow either?"

Thongden shrugged. "You could decide not to see her," he said coldly. "But that would be an interference with what has already been established."

"Then I should see her," I said.

"Certainly you should not," Thongden persisted. "'Should' is also an interference. Do not interfere with anything now set in motion. Let everything be. Do you understand?"

By now I was beginning to feel very tired. My youthful buoyancy had faded. I raised my fingers to my forehead. It was still smooth. "Just one thing," I said. "Will I remain young like this?"

"How can you ask," he said, "when nothing is yet established? Consider only that there is nothing to be done. *That,* perhaps, is hardest of all to do."

"What about breathing exercises?"

"Why would you need them now—when you have nothing more to do?" And suddenly he bathed me in the iciest smile I had yet received from him. I settled back uneasily on the couch and heard myself murmuring my final question: "Do you know anything about foxes?"

"That's a strange question," I heard Thongden say. I felt relieved at his answer. Thongden didn't know everything after all.

And then I fell asleep. And I had another dream. I was flying over Manhattan, carrying Louise in my arms, and I had the feeling that I had just rescued her from some great danger. We were passing fairly low over the second World Trade Center building when I noticed Thongden on the observation platform waving his fist at me. As we passed overhead I heard him shout, "No—you cannot. You must not."

I remember nothing more until I awoke. It was late morning. The sun was streaming through the eastern windows of the room. There was no sign of Thongden. I looked at my watch. Eleven o'clock. I needed to wash, straighten my clothing, and grab some coffee up on Broadway somewhere. And it could still take me up to an hour to get to the Bronx Zoo, maybe another half hour to find my way to the foxes. But I didn't even stop to ask myself whether I should go. I simply had no choice.

Louise had arrived ahead of me. As I came up the path, I could see her stooping low at the railing, reaching her hands through to pet the red fox. This time there was a second fox that hung back a bit. It was somewhat smaller, probably the female of the pair. Louise was still wearing the turquoise earrings, but she wore a dark skirt pulled in tightly at the waist with a white lace blouse tucked inside. The blouse had shortened sleeves that reached just below the elbows. Today she had added a turquoise ring on the index finger of her right hand and a turquoise bracelet just above her watchband. She looked like a schoolgirl.

"Hi," I said tentatively, feeling schoolboyish myself in my delight at seeing her.

Without saying anything she raised a hand toward me, which I grasped, pulling her to her feet. The touch of her fingers brought everything back again. We faced each other. Again we went through that ceremony of searching each other with our eyes. To my happy surprise, it still worked. There was really something between us that went to the roots.

"Were you waiting long?" I managed.

"Not really. But—it seemed long."

"Have you finished your colloquy with Reynard?" I asked.

The fox was still standing near the fence, watching her. "I don't think I should spoil him anymore," she said. "Where would you like to go?"

We had started walking again, our hands still locked together. "Do you live near here?"

"Near enough," she said vaguely.

"Do you always get off from work this early?"

"I pretty much make my own hours."

"That's very nice. What do you do?"

She shrugged, looked at me with what I thought an evasive expression. Then, as I remained turned toward her, waiting for a reply, she said, "I'm a personal companion."

"To an elderly person?"

"No."

A thought stabbed at me. "A man?"

"Oh no. A woman."

"I see."

"An invalid?"

"She's a young woman, like me."

"Really?"

"You think that's strange?"

"I really don't know. Why—?"

"What do you do?" she said.

"I'm a writer."

And then, with the next question, which was the one I normally get asked almost every time and for which I usually had a simple answer, I found myself caught in a dilemma. "What kind of writing do you do?"

"Books—novels—and I used to write—" And I stopped before the word "Superman" escaped my lips. When was "used to" and when was "now"? How could I have written Superman in the '40s and '50s unless I was over seventy?

"What were you going to say?" she asked.

"I used to write—poetry," I said. It was the truth. I had actually had some poetry published in my teens. That was so very long ago, it was safe. "You know," I said, steering the conversation into an even more precarious direction, knowing I had better not and knowing also that I simply had to, "have you thought any more about—us?"

She squeezed my hand more tightly while she kept her eyes straight ahead on the path. "I thought about it all night," she confessed.

"And—?"

She withdrew her hand and raised her shoulders in a gesture of futility. "What about you?"

"It's very strange," I admitted. "The connection feels strong. And yet—" I turned to face her, almost ready to tell her the truth but not daring to strain her credulity, convinced I'd lose her completely if I did, "it wasn't a small thing," I said weakly. "I don't understand how we can both feel that way and not remember."

She took my hand again and offered me a tentative smile. "Even so—it's such a grand feeling—like floating in applesauce—isn't it?"

That brought a loud, solid laugh out of me. It was literally a delicious metaphor. And it instantly dispelled a lingering awkwardness between us. "If I'd let myself think of it that way from the beginning," I confessed, "I might not have found it so unnerving."

"You mean—scary?"

"Well—sure. So beyond the normal."

"Love is always beyond the normal," she said. The word warmed me as it fell from her lips. I wouldn't have dared to utter the word "love" to her. Yet that was exactly what I felt. Now, at least, I could say it to myself. I was in love with her.

"Sometimes," she suggested, "things happen between two people —that maybe hurt so much that they just can't remember. But because they still care—"

Her girlish attempt at psychologizing charmed me. But then, how could she have known what I knew—that if we really *had* met before in some way, it was in a dimension of time she couldn't have known about? But anxious as I was to learn more about her so I could come to grips with the mystery of any previous relationship, I was ready to abandon even that just for the sheer joy of her presence in that moment of ardent revelation. It was, I realized, an utterly different kind of experience for me—the satisfaction in just being close to her, holding hands with her, bound to her by that strong sense of belonging together despite our ignorance of its origin. We were simply there for each other. And it was very real—a time mysteriously torn out of the fabric of possibility. One of the wonderful unpromised surprises of life.

I write rhapsodically about it because it was rhapsodic. We walked, we held hands, we prattled generalities about ourselves to each other. I talked about writing, she about her growing-up years in French-speaking northern New Brunswick. I wondered about the odd gaps in her story. It was like reading a book from which chapters were missing. She must have had similar questions about me. Yet we both knew that in some way, right there, as we walked and picnicked in the park and visited the various animal sections, we were sharing as much as it's ever possible to share out of the full flower of youth.

At the end of the day, when she suddenly decided it was time for her to leave, we both understood that we would meet again at the foxes on the following afternoon.

* * *

Once more I returned to Thongden's. There was no point in returning to northern Westchester since Kay wouldn't be back for some
days yet, and after all our years of being together I had come to hate
an empty house. On the other hand, I was grateful for her absence.
This was not a time when I would have wanted to explain what was
going on with me.

Thongden had obviously been expecting me. He had not only
had the couch made up more comfortably for me, with a fresh sheet
and pillowcase, but he even had a Reuben sandwich waiting for me
in the food warmer in the kitchen.

"I did everything I could to pander to your comfort and your
gustatory vices," he remarked, bringing the sandwich out for me on
a tray. I thanked him and noticed that he looked a little different
tonight. He was wearing a plain sort of kimono and a pair of oriental thong slippers. And he looked a little pale, almost as though a
certain opacity had been lost. But he had never been more gracious
to me.

I used his bathroom for a quick shower, then settled on the
couch with my sandwich, half expecting him to question me about
the day's events. To my surprise, he brought up a different subject
altogether. He began discussing certain aspects of his long relationship with Nelson.

"I did not tell you that after our meeting in that village, when
Rimpoche Nelson decided not to dissolve me—we never saw each
other again."

"But you said you kept in touch. That he was actually your guru
through all those years."

Thongden nodded and squatted down on some cushions in front
of the couch. "All true. We never lost contact. Being of the same
mind substance, we had only to allow ourselves to be enfolded in the
wholeness and we could communicate."

"You said it wasn't telepathy," I reminded him.

"Telepathy was not necessary. Our fundamental unity was there whenever we chose to pass out of individual manifestation. So I learned whatever he learned and wished me to learn. And then I would separate myself, living my own life but exercising in that life what he had taught me."

I thought about this for a moment. "What if he had dissolved you, then? Would it really have made much difference? You would still have been together."

Thongden was about to reply but waited while I paused to bite into my sandwich. He watched me with a strange half smile. "It is better that the food and the eater be separate," he remarked.

"Why?"

He tittered. "There is more pleasure in it."

"Hm—you don't object to pleasure, then?"

"Should one object to the dance of life?"

Another thought occurred to me. "What would he have had to do to dissolve you?"

"Ah—you think he just did not want to take the trouble?"

"Oh no—just curious. How would he have done it?"

Thongden shrugged. "By reunifying with me."

"Sounds simple enough. Is it?"

He shook his head. "It requires a leap of thought. To leap requires a great advance flexing of the muscles, a pulling back and then a sharp thrust. All in the mind. But the mind," he added, tapping himself just below the chest, "in here. The great center of feeling."

"I would have thought," I said, "that it was always preferable to return to the source. To rejoin the infinite, if I may extend the metaphor. Isn't that what all Eastern religions try for?"

He raised his arms, holding his palms up and out. "Do not disdain the humble dot," he said, referring once more to the contents of the cylinder with the crank.

I recognized another of his paradoxes, but I was already too tired to think about it any further. Now, too, he seemed to turn away from me and become absorbed in thoughts of his own. I recognized his wish for silence and put aside my own wish to ask him further questions about my experiences with Louise. I still could not escape the feeling that he was changing. A certain warmth was gone, and every now and then, unexpectedly, I would catch a glint in his eyes that looked like pure malevolence. I remembered Madame David-Neel's experience. Was this something that overtook all *tulpa*s? Were they so much less firmly rooted in the material world that a moody capriciousness tended to overtake them after a time? But, I reminded myself, Thongden had been around for many years. Why would he suddenly begin to change now? Maybe he and I were less compatible than he and Nelson had been. Perhaps I lacked something essential that his stability required. I had no way of knowing. But there was nothing I could do about it anyway. I couldn't begin to understand how to dissolve him, and he had started things going in my own psyche for which I was now prepared to risk a great deal if he would only help me reach a clearer understanding. I was willing to pay the price as he prescribed it so far. And that, at this moment, meant holding to the requirement for nonaction.

I finished my sandwich, used the washroom to brush my teeth, and returned to find that he had darkened the room considerably and gone into deep meditation. I curled up on the couch and fell asleep. This time I had no dreams that I could remember.

Chapter Twenty

In spite of my youthful physical appearance and the extra energy that came with it, my tastes and outlook and philosophy belonged to my true age. That was still my reality. My bodily alteration ultimately went no deeper than providing an outer garment for a personality essentially unchanged. If I had altered the time dimension and still left my basic self intact, then perhaps time itself was merely a husk, an epiphenomenon that had no capacity to affect my essential selfhood. I had no clear answer to that question, but it led me to wonder how a man with the outlook of mature years could continue the interminable circuit of hand-holding and melting sighs and yearning—walking round and round the park with a young lady who at her very best possessed maturity just a shade above adolescence.

How could she have been otherwise? She was a young woman of nineteen or twenty. And I listened to her, adored her, and hung on her jejune comments and vision of the world with unbroken fascination and interest and more than a little nostalgia. Perhaps it was all merely a biological function so that the male of the species would remain forever smitten by the genes of youth, regardless of time and condition, and so that wisdom, if age can be presumed to possess some of that rare attribute, had little relevance when the fundamental DNA presented its own demands. Whatever was causing it, and however absurd it seemed, I was, as they say, smitten.

I continued to walk with her, listen to her, glow in her presence, and pine when she was not around, and it didn't matter how little of consequence we had to say to each other. When our eyes met we were lost in the depths of our gazes. And yet, as though somehow confuting the DNA's own requirements, we never went beyond that surface fascination. There was not only no sex between us, I did not even feel impelled to make sexual advances. Sexual feelings were unmistakably there but sublimated in what was apparently the endless ritual of a long courtship. Perhaps that kind of courtship is something innate among humans that our contemporary culture and civilization has somehow lost. Perhaps such a prolonged courtship, if it is indeed the truly natural way, might make for longer and stronger postnuptial ties. Again, I had no way of knowing. But it did seem at times as though the little we knew about each other, far from being an impediment to our mutual attraction, only seemed to strengthen it, providing in some way an otherness more powerful than any other and explaining to some small degree that mysterious magnetism that sometimes seems strongest when a man and a woman are strangers to each other.

I would speculate on these things when I was away from her. I found myself immersed in the sheer joy of her presence when we were together. I do not know how long this strange relationship would have continued, but the time was approaching when Kay would return from Canada and my daily trysts with Louise would have to come to an end. However, I had, as I said, accepted Thongden's dictum about nonacting action. I intended to let this thing carry on by itself without any interference from me. With all that had happened so far, I was hardly likely to question Thongden's certainty on this point.

In the meantime our walks extended in an ever widening circuit of the park, which actually covers some 252 acres. One day, having wandered through the building housing the cages of the great cats, we reached the outer edge of the park. On a large barren adjacent lot just outside the gates, the structural steel shaft of a giant crane jutted far above the great oaks at the park's outer edge. We came to a narrow dirt path, probably used by zoo personnel for some purpose or other, which came to a dead end at a heavy chain-link fence. Looking through, we noticed that on the vast stretch of meadow beyond the park the tents of what appeared to be a traveling carnival were being set up. Circus wagons were parked about; there were men and women in work clothes and a man in a clown suit. Groups of mobile cages were being assembled, and the giant crane, which stood at the center of the whole affair, was somehow being used to assist in the rapid assembly of the parts.

"Looks like a traveling carnival," I said.

"I didn't know there was such a big meadow on this side of the park," Louise said. "I remember there used to be high-rise buildings here for low-income families."

"They've been tearing those things down," I said. "It's a pretty scraggly-looking meadow."

"Do you like carnivals?" she said.

"When I was younger—" I had been about to mention something of my younger courting days when I caught myself. "As a kid I used to go with my parents."

"The rides should be up by tomorrow," Louise said. "Will you take me?"

"Do you really want to go?" I said, not finding the prospect especially enticing.

"Oh yes. I love carnivals."

"That settles it. What you love, I love," I assured her.

It was late again. We agreed to meet at the usual place the next day and then leave the park from the other side to reach the carnival.

* * *

Because it was a Friday, a late extra commuter train was scheduled that would get me to the central switching point at Harmon Station, where I could transfer to a train to Peekskill and a short cab ride home. Once aboard I found myself in a comfortable no-man's land, looking out the train window and watching Manhattan recede into Spuyten Duyvil and then following the slow run along the Hudson River and the rocky cliffs of the Palisades on the farther shore. This particular commute had served me for years and constituted a kind of private haven where, alone with my thoughts, somewhere in between the locus of work and business in Manhattan and the locus of home and family in Westchester, I often felt most at one with myself and most comfortably alone.

On this particular trip I finally felt free of the influence of Thongden and the heady, congested buildup of feeling that marked my long meetings with Louise. It was as though I had stepped out of a world that, from this quiet haven of a train, seemed both eerie and extrinsic to my real life. I found myself longing for the mundane, the ordinary, the unimaginative. Underneath the semblance of youth that I still carried about like a heavy cloak, I had a yearning for my good established life with Kay—the old pair of slippers and cozy recliner existence. And suddenly, as I sat there, I began to laugh at the absurdity of thinking I could ever have had or wished for such a quiet, somnolent type of existence. More to the point, I realized with a certain sense of foreboding, was the fact that the events of the last few weeks were now all about to come to a head, that Superman figured in some mysterious way, and that connected with Superman was everything else—Thongden, Louise, Kay, and my own mysterious and protean selfhood. And I could do nothing at all except wait for events to assume the shape the universe dictated.

The first part of the reshaping happened after I got back to the house. There were messages on my answering machine. One was from Hedy Greene, wondering if I had any new ideas for her. The second was from Kay. She was tired of being away from home; she missed my solid presence and occasional lunacies and was bored to tears with our grown-up suburban children. So she was rushing back. I was to expect her the next afternoon. What would she find when she got here? Her familiar, aging Alvin or a young man she didn't know or would scarcely remember? I tried not to think too much about that. Not now.

The third was from Thongden. Not since he first contacted me—when, mistaking him for a fan, I cut him off—had I received a phone call from Thongden. There was something especially foreboding about this call—as though it were his last.

"It will all come together now. Just as you have known all along. If you continue not to interfere, you will have no further need of me. Yours in eternal unity—Thongden."

I played this message over several times, thinking to myself that I did indeed know. It had filled my thoughts on the train coming home. I knew the denouement was at hand, and these messages all confirmed that. But I didn't know what the resolution could possibly be. What I did know was that it would at first be fragile, that if I took a wrong step or tried to interfere in any way I would set in train a thousand new possibilities, postponing the denouement again—perhaps for good. I knew I had to be very watchful because I had to come to the end of this process. Life on Thongden's Path without Form could only be endured for so long. Would I end up as myself again? Or as myself long ago? The latter prospect, despite its temptations, was too disturbing to contemplate, especially when I thought of Kay.

I slept in my own bed that night. But I slept fitfully. Fugitive dreams kept disturbing my rest, and I woke several times with a feeling that I was not alone in my bedroom. But of course I wasn't. I never really had been. All the phantasms that had been built up around my life had always been with me, but I had never before been so aware of them. Most of all I was aware of two presences, Superman and Thongden, and they seemed to intermingle bewilderingly, each shifting through and becoming the other as my dreaming self tried to come to grips with them. At no time did I have a single thought of Louise.

The next morning I shaved—the full ritual, which I had not done for many years. I put on my most casual clothes. I wore a pair of old jeans and a blue workshirt that I had buried in my dresser some time ago after they became a little tight for me. But this morning they presented no problem for my younger self. I wore my Reeboks instead of my regular shoes. It was, I felt, appropriate garb for taking an eager late teen to a carnival, and I found that the old feeling had returned. I was again looking forward to seeing her. This feeling was tempered by a kind of sadness at the realization that it might be for the last time. For that reason alone, I knew our meeting would be memorable.

It was—right from the start when I met her at the foxes. She was waiting for me. Before I could say a word to her, she threw her arms around me and kissed me with warm, wet, uncompromising lips, right there on the path, oblivious of the few passersby who came that way. I felt a moment of terror and guilt, immediately followed by the sensation of drowning in bliss. I felt the wonder of being twenty years old again all the way down through my tensile second-time-around body. When she tried to break away I held on to her just a little longer. Finally she stepped back, her cheeks glowing red.

"I had to do that," she said breathlessly. "All this time we are together, and you have never even tried to kiss me." She was so emotional that her English had regressed into its original Acadian inflections. "I know you want to kiss me. But you are the shyest man I have ever met. Maybe I like you for that too. But you must not be shy anymore."

I immediately took her at her word and kissed her again. When I released her, she took my hand. "Come," she said. "Let's go to the carnival."

This was not exactly the way I had envisioned things working out. But what I had done, I had done spontaneously. So far I had not interfered.

Chapter Twenty-One

To get to the carnival, we would have had to exit the park and go all the way around to the other side, a distance of about a mile. We decided to take a cab.

Either they had worked overnight or the carnival workers were very fast. Everything was up and running, and visitors were shuffling around the various exhibits. What I had mistaken for the shaft of a giant crane turned out to be the axis around which hung a fleet of small two-seater airplanes that slowly climbed the shaft while circling it in an ever widening orbit propelled by centrifugal force and held by a pair of expanding hydraulic arms. Then it began to speed up. It was the most spectacular ride in the whole carnival, and certainly one of the highest and fastest I ever remembered seeing. I noticed that every seat was occupied in the miniature planes, from each of which hands were waving in apparent glee and excitement.

"What a ride," I said, gazing upward nervously.

"You like it?" said Louise. She sounded much too eager.

"Like it?" I repeated. "Not even from down here on the ground."

"You don't like it?" she said, sounding disappointed. "We're not going?"

"I'd be terrified," I assured her. I wasn't just reacting with an old man's caution. Even as a kid I had probably been the most reluctant customer that ever ventured on board a roller coaster.

"But," Louise insisted, hugging me, "you mustn't worry. I'll protect you. With me you'll never be nervous for one minute. Come—it'll be good for you."

I pulled back. "Look—all my life I've had a thing about heights. I'm a sedentary type. A writer. Remember? I even get uncomfortable in fast elevators."

She laughed, refusing to take me seriously. "Then for me you will be even more of a hero." She kept tugging at my arm. I still resisted, but feebly. I didn't want to break the noninterference rule by opposing too forcefully. And I didn't want to step up onto that ticket platform where she was leading me. Caught in this odd dilemma, the notion that anything decisive could be looming here for either of us suddenly seemed too absurd to entertain. The whole thing was plain silly. My resistance flagged. I let her pull me onto the platform, where I bought two tickets.

"I hope you realize," I told her, "that I don't have a heroic bone in my body. But for you—I'm even willing to change that."

She squeezed my arm and gave me a quick kiss on the cheek. "I knew right away you were a wonderful man," she said.

"I hope," I said, holding her arm as she stepped aboard one of the waiting craft and took her seat, "they didn't put these things up so fast that they left out important parts, like connecting bolts and stuff." I stepped gingerly onto the slightly swaying contraption and took my seat beside her. She put an arm around my waist and I slung mine tightly around her shoulders. The music began, blaring its mind-stunning beat from a pair of giant metal speakers right there on the platform, drowning out our voices. As the ride got under way, carrying us away from the platform, we began to climb at a slight and not too uncomfortable rate.

Then, with a sudden lurch, we began to rise and swing outward, away from the supporting shaft. I glanced down toward the ground and happened, amid the milling and flow of visitors, to see a large, heavily muscled man wearing some kind of bright tank-top shirt and a pair of colorful red and blue clown pants moving toward the platform from which we had just risen. He looked as if he might have been an employee doing double duty as a clown and a strongman who had at the same time been called into service as a repairman. He was carrying what looked like an enormous box wrench, with which I saw him disappear under the platform where the machinery operating our ride was housed. But at the very point of that disappearance, for a mere fraction of a second, I saw him look up and caught just a glimpse of such malignity on his face that it staggered me—perhaps even more than the shock of recognizing the face of Thongden. In a strange way, aware as I was of the *tulpa*'s predilection for disguise, the recognition did not surprise me. In any case my surprise was smothered in a terror created by the certainty that we were facing disaster. In the next moment I understood completely that there really was nothing I could do. It was too late. And too far gone. There was no point even in trying to tell Louise. In what way could she have prepared herself, except by tensing up and possibly being more seriously injured when the crash came? And I knew that was about to happen very soon.

I tilted my head up, trying to see the upper part of the supporting shaft, whose tip seemed to reach into the sun. At the same time I could feel the centrifugal force pushing against my body as we spiraled with increasing speed up and around the shaft. I clung even more tightly to Louise's shoulder.

Then I looked down again. We were two-thirds of the way up the shaft. Below I saw the man in the clown suit—I could see now for certain that it was Thongden—emerge hurriedly from beneath the platform. Something seemed to be bothering him; he started waving his box wrench around and yelling at the bystanders as they gradually inched back away from the platform. I braced myself. And then I felt it—a slight irregularity—a snapping disposition in the motion of our toy plane, as though somewhere a cog wheel had missed. We seemed, as I glanced about, to be at a slightly different inclination from the shaft than the other planes around us. I felt a clear certainty that we were about to shake loose. Louise noticed nothing, her eyes squeezed shut in supreme glee, her fingers digging into my waist as though she were getting ready to release everything and fly off fearlessly into another dimension. "Didn't you feel that?" I shouted at her over the noise of the rising music.

She shook her head, her eyes still closed, a smile of delight on her features.

"We're in trouble," I exclaimed.

Again she shook her head. I knew she had actually felt that snapping motion, which was now repeating itself along with a series of sudden shudders. "It's—so—exciting," she gasped, still smiling.

"My God," I exclaimed in utter exasperation. "Who are you?"

Her eyes opened. She looked at me. I could have sworn I heard her say very distinctly, "Ask Kay." But of course that was impossible. Besides, it was now happening—sheer catastrophe. I could see the entire shaft that held all of us tilting slowly over in a great arc. I heard screams from the other planes. We were beginning to fall.

Just a few times in my life I have had the experience of onrushing, imminent, and inescapable danger. Once in my early twenties I tried to pass a car on a two-lane highway when an oncoming pickup suddenly loomed up in the lane before me. My brakes failed. I couldn't draw back behind the vehicle I was passing. I could only sit there in some unending suspension of time, my foot pressed on the useless brake, awaiting the instant of total destruction. Then, at the very last fragment of time, it seemed, some part of my brake locked, just enough to generate an uneven pull on the wheels that sent my vehicle skidding onto the far left shoulder in a half turn as the onrushing pickup poured suddenly through the spot I had just vacated. I never got over the feeling that a powerful force, like some mighty hand, had reached out of eternity and snatched me back to life. I had other experiences like it—two others, to be exact. But what strikes me about such moments is that while they are happening, time itself seems to change. It's as though, faced with destruction, the mind gets so speeded up that the threatening event seems to take far longer than it actually does. This allows for almost endless moments of clear thinking, perhaps because of an inner safety mechanism that tries to provide a way out right up to the final nanosecond.

That's what it seemed like in that little plane. I could see the shaft tilting over on its way to the ground. I could see my little plane and all the others around me swinging erratically out of orbit. I could feel my mind ripping through a thousand thoughts. Of these, the very first was that I had surely known this would happen. Then there was the thought that this was part of that movement of the universe that Thongden had promised would resolve everything. And finally I realized that this particular resolution, being forever removed from the universe by death, did not meet with my approval and that it was time I interfered to prevent it.

I don't even know how the thought of being able to interfere arose at that point when, clearly, it was too late to do anything. But it led instantly into another complicated notion that the exceptional speed of my mind at the moment allowed me to follow all the way to the end. I remembered all of my recent experiments in consciousness transference. I recalled my having plunged into the consciousness of an ostrich. How I had followed this feat by lining myself up with a mass consciousness of small birds. And then how I had found my way into the consciousness of a fly. I recalled these events while at least half a dozen other thoughts rushed by in equal clarity. And here I was still bound into the physical body of youth, my old man's material body lost in some space-time lacuna that was neither yesterday nor today. I had done all these things, I reminded myself, and needed only one further step, the defining one, to tie all the subsequent ones together—the materialization of Superman.

According to Thongden, I had already created a partial *tulpa*. But my thoughts of Superman had never been sufficiently concentrated to make him visible to anyone except someone like Thongden. Perhaps too he was visible to people who had the gift of seeing auras. I even knew people like that, but I had never had anyone walk up to me and say, "Hey—you've got a Superman aura following you around." Of course the problem at this present moment of extreme emergency was to complete the materialization of Superman.

But what would that do? Would Superman immediately proceed to rescue us? Maybe he'd try to save someone else. Maybe he'd just go off somewhere and not bother. I mean—once he became independent—a true *tulpa*—he might just run away, as Thongden had done.

Suddenly I remembered the Path without Form and Thongden explaining how from the *inside* one could remain in control. I had done it with the fly. But could I do the same with the complex personality I had formed out of Superman?

I knew the answer almost at once. *From the inside everything is connected.* And here I was on the inside. And I was making the leap of thought he mentioned. From the inside I was just as much Superman as Alvin.

Then I was really making the leap, transferring consciousness once again.

I don't know if I can describe it completely. First there was the supreme effort to visualize Superman so that I could see him, at least with my inner eye. I made, you might say, an imaginative pattern of him. Understand, this was not just a pretty mind picture. This involved, as Thongden had advised, an advance flexing of the muscles, a pulling back that I now realized was like an archer feeding power into a drawn bow, a youthful, adrenaline-charged warrior compacting all the energy I could gather as I focused my strength against the terrible pressure of that threatening moment. There was, above all, some greater and more mysterious power that recent events had awakened in me. I do believe that for an instant Superman actually became visible not only to me but to others. I caught a glimpse of Louise staring off into space, her eyes fixed on some point no more than a few yards from our erratically careening airplane. So she must have been seeing him too. But the main thing now was to reabsorb him, draw him into myself just as he was, with all his own energy and otherworldly capacity—precisely as visualized. I made a supreme effort. And I felt a jolt.

What happened next took place in some vacuum of awareness in which my consciousness was not fully in one place or another. To explain it I have to borrow from the philosopher Martin Buber describing a condition of being in the consciousness of a tree and in his human consciousness at the same time. He spoke of leaning on a stick that he had pressed against the tree. In his words, "I felt the stick at both ends."

Similarly, I felt the fall of our plane being cushioned, then eased slowly down, while at the same time I felt myself bracing the collapsing shaft, all fifty tons of buckling steel, and lowering it gently to the ground. Then I found myself standing on the outside of a small crowd that had gathered around. They were watching people, unhurt, scrambling from the little planes splayed all about. I had apparently left my seat in the plane at some indeterminate point. And I felt as though, magically, I had flown down. I caught a glimpse of Louise lifting herself from her seat, looking vaguely about as though she had forgotten something. Then she turned, and her gaze fell precisely on me as I stood watching her. That was when I saw her repeat the routine she had gone through when our eyes first met at the restaurant in the park. A glimmer of recognition followed by a frown, a moment of confusion, and then a quick turning away. Involuntarily my hand rose to my face. The first thing I felt was my beard. Reaching a little higher, I felt the old familiar furrows of age on my forehead.

I felt a spasm of disappointment. And then came sudden unaccountable elation. In that moment I understood something else. I understood the mysterious silence of Superman.

Chapter Twenty-Two

Kay was already home by the time I got back. She had specifically asked me not to meet her at the airport. She wanted to settle into her house by herself and just be alone for a while—a luxury she hadn't been able to enjoy during the visit to our daughter and granddaughter.

I didn't know quite what to expect when I got home, but I was getting used to the unexpected ever since Thongden had first appeared in my life a couple of months earlier. I also had to deal with another major difficulty on seeing Kay. I was now convinced that at that last terrifying moment on the carnival ride, when I turned to Louise in exasperation and said, "Who are you?" she had replied, "Ask Kay."

I had doubted that she really said it simply because I couldn't believe there could be any connection. So I assumed I had misheard. But as I began to go over all the strange connections that had already occurred and to search the memory of that final moment in the miniature plane with Louise, I knew that she very clearly had said, "Ask Kay."

Simple—all I had to do was "ask Kay." Just like that. And at the same time tell her all about Louise. After forty-five years of one of those truly rare faithful marriages, how was I going to bring up Louise at all? I would rather have stuck my head in the mouth of that huge Bengal tiger Louise and I had watched a few times during our endless circuits of the zoo. Not that Kay would have made a terrible fuss. That wasn't her way. She'd accept it as part of the strange events that had recently entered our lives. But it would hurt just the same. And I couldn't bear to hurt her.

And yet—I had to know what "Ask Kay" meant. Somehow it was a crucial element in the whole experience. Maybe if I first explained very carefully about the Path without Form and how one is really lost on it and—damn it. No. I simply couldn't handle it. Not yet anyhow.

Fortunately there were a few other unexpected matters that diverted our attention by the time I got home. After the hugs and the questions about the kids and was the trip comfortable and the normal amenities of homecoming, Kay announced, "There was something about Superman in the morning paper. Did you hear?"

"Superman? Well—I mean—that's not so unusual, is it? He still gets his share of publicity."

But I already guessed it had something to do with the rescue at the carnival. I waited uncomfortably for Kay to tell me the rest. Had anything happened to connect me to Louise?

"At this carnival somewhere in the Bronx," she confirmed. "One of the high rides collapsed. But—miraculously—no one got hurt. One eyewitness says he saw a figure in a Superman costume come out of nowhere and grab this fifty-ton steel support shaft and lower it and everybody else on the ride safely to the ground."

"One witness?" I said.

"Well—there was also a woman who reported seeing someone like Superman, but she couldn't be sure. She said she kind of saw it but was sure she just imagined it. A couple of others also thought they saw Superman."

"I see."

"There was a reporter there too. He explained that one of the ground crew—a big man who doubled as a clown and as a carnival strongman—he was the one that did it."

"Did what?"

"Caught the shaft and brought it to a safe landing."

"What did the man say?"

"Well—he waved his arms in front of the camera. He said 'sure' he saved the ride. He could hardly speak English. But he insisted that he'd broken the fall of the shaft. Although he didn't explain how he managed to fly up there to do it."

"I'll bet."

"Anyway, the reporter pointed out that the man had on part of his clown costume. Something very colorful—easily mistaken for Superman. And of course the reporter said it couldn't have been Superman."

"Why not?"

Kay smiled. "Because Superman isn't real. He's a comic book character—remember?"

I settled into my favorite easy chair and looked up at her. "Of course. A comic book character."

"On the other hand," Kay said, "I thought it might have been *your* Superman."

"Did you now?" I said, beginning to feel uncomfortable again.

To my surprise, she came and sat on the arm of my chair. "When I was away all that time, I was able to think clearly. I finally realized that your Mr. Thongden couldn't have been just a fan of yours. That maybe he really was a *tulpa*. Also, Naomi passed on some interesting Indian lore that made me think twice."

Naomi had told her some stories about creatures like *tulpa*s in Indian legend and that certain older Indians whom she had come to know during later visits to the reserve had actually encountered such beings. So Kay had acquired some reinforcement for accepting my claims about Thongden.

"And that means," I said with an air of satisfaction, "that you're even willing to accord Superman a somewhat equivalent status?"

"I know you and Thongden were having those visits at the zoo. It *was* your Superman, wasn't it?"

"That's just the tip of the iceberg," I told her.

"I'm still a long way from understanding what you call reality, Alvin," she admitted. "By the way, did you have anything to eat yet?"

I now discovered I was hungry. She went into the kitchen to prepare something. I sat there listening to her bustling around. "Can I help?" I finally called in.

"Yes," she called back.

I got up and stood in the kitchen doorway. "Ready, willing, and able," I said.

"No—I mean help with reality. I can manage the food. I need help with reality."

"I know. But right now?"

"Do you think you can tell me now who turns the crank?"

I stared at her. Then I thought about it for a few moments. Finally I said, "Let's eat first. Then I'll try to get it all in order."

Kay has a little trick for turning rounds of pita bread, tomato paste, and low-fat cheese flavored with an imitation all-cereal sausage into a pizza of sorts. We were both caught up in the anticholesterol battle and hadn't yet discovered any way of transferring our magical experiences into the gustatory realm. But that night we sat around our big circular table and did our best to enjoy what we had while I tried to explain the magic of recent events with Thongden, particularly the breathing exercises and the whole business of consciousness transference. I told her about becoming an ostrich, a flock of birds, a bunch of animals, an old lady, and a fly. I made no mention of Louise. She listened to me carefully, ate slowly, and said nothing.

"Does your silence mean you're not buying it?"

"My silence means I feel there's something important being left out," she said.

I should have realized that after forty-five years of marriage, I really didn't have a place left to hide from her.

"Like what?" I said.

"Like Superman. How did Superman get to that carnival? You hate carnivals. What were you doing there?"

"Oh, that," I said. "Well—it started back a few days. Maybe a week or so. I had this dream when we were first going by cab to the Bronx Zoo."

"You and Thongden?"

I nodded. "Yes—me and Thongden. I fell asleep on him. And I had this dream about Superman." And then I told her how I'd dreamed of Superman saving the Queensborough Bridge and how he came back to the cab and just sat there not saying a word, and how Thongden agreed that Superman's silence in the dream was important.

"Important how?" Kay said, watching me closely.

"I didn't know. Not until he turned up at the carnival."

"How did he happen to turn up?"

I knew then that it was over. There was no way I could explain anything without telling her about Louise. "Look," I said, getting up. "Let's go over and sit down there." I indicated my favorite armchair, which faced her own favorite corner of the couch. I felt somehow that the whole thing would go down better if we were both in our most effectively padded places. She seemed to understand and without another word got up and walked over to the couch and settled in her favorite spot. I walked to my armchair, but I didn't sit. Somehow I had to do this thing standing up.

Without looking at her directly, I told about the first time I'd seen Louise, noting that she showed some sign of recognizing me and then seemed to change her mind. Then about how I became a fly and how, after that, I had the miraculous transformation and became twenty years old.

"Now I know this is absolutely, totally unbelievable," I declared. "But this is where our notions of reality come in. This is where it becomes clear that reality isn't just a fixed something that we can lay our hands on, Kay. It's plastic, changeable—" I stopped suddenly. She was looking at me in a funny way.

"What is it?" I asked.

"This girl—describe her again."

Puzzled, I described what Louise had been wearing. I described her short black hair, her earrings—and then stopped as I saw Kay's eyes widen. She seemed to press back further in her corner seat.

"Did you say they were turquoise earrings?"

"Yes—the dangle kind. Why?"

"Are you sure they were turquoise?"

"Of course I'm sure."

"Anything else?" Kay said. There was a faint tremor in her voice.

"Anything else—what?"

"Any other jewelry?"

"Oh—she had this wristwatch. I guess you'd call it jewelry because of the turquoise band. Why?"

"Oh my God—my God," Kay murmured. She seemed to be speaking to herself. Her eyes were really wide now.

"I don't know why it's so important," I said, mystified. "But when I met her later on—there were other turquoise things. I remember a ring and a bracelet and—well, she was kind of a nut on turquoise. I remember when we met at the foxes' cage—"

Kay half rose from her seat. "What about foxes?" she exclaimed.

"Hey—what's wrong? Are you all right?"

She brushed a hand across her face and straightened in her seat. I could see she was trying to get a grip on herself. "Did she have a—pet fox?"

"Well—" I admitted. "Sort of." I explained about the fox she'd made friends with at the zoo. Kay was very pale. She got even paler when I told her how Louise had spoken to the fox in French. It was clear enough by now that Kay had her own mysterious connection with Louise. I asked her point-blank.

"It can't be a coincidence," she said, standing up now and looking at me with eyes opened wider than ever.

"Maybe it's your turn to tell me," I said.

"No—not yet. I've got to be sure. Please—do you mind?"

"Well—all right," I said, watching her with growing concern.

Kay began to ask me questions—detailed questions. She wanted to know exactly how Louise's hair fell behind her ears. She asked about eye color. About makeup. About whether she had a high, rounded forehead. How tall was she? Did she have very smooth hands? Were they large or small? I couldn't answer all of her questions, but I answered enough to know that we were talking about a person we both knew. But how?

"Look," I said. "This is getting to me. I can't stand the suspense anymore. Tell me who Louise is."

"It's scary," Kay said.

"It's reality," I insisted, even now trying to get my point in.

"All right. Sit down." She pointed to my chair and took up her own seat again. "Years ago—early '40s, that's when it was. When I left home for the first time. I took the train to Montreal all the way from Bathurst. I'd never been that far from home before. I was only eighteen."

"I know about that," I said.

"I was supposed to stay with my older sister. You remember that, don't you?"

I nodded.

"But Arnolda had just been married. I felt I was just in the way. I had a little money saved, so I got a room of my own in the Notre Dame de Grace section. I told you about that. I was so scared and lonely. I was so confused by the big city. And frightened. I'd never even seen a black person before. And I was afraid to talk to anyone."

"I remember you telling me all of this," I said.

Kay took a deep breath. "Well—you know how children some-times invent an imaginary playmate to keep them company?"

"Sure—I remember doing something like that once myself. Before my brother was born."

"Well—that's what I did. I invented an imaginary playmate. I invented *your* lady friend from the park. To keep me company. She was like my invisible Barbie doll. I dressed her. I gave her that thick black hair because my hair was always so fine and unmanageable."

"And you made her an Acadian with Micmac Indian blood and then covered her with turquoise jewelry as though she were a Navajo from New Mexico? Talk about being inconsistent."

Kay shrugged. "I just liked turquoise. And what did I know about Navajos? I knew about Micmacs from down home. And—yes—I always wanted a pet fox, but Daddy said it was impossible to domes-ticate a fox. So I gave one to *her*."

Suddenly I started to laugh.

"What's so funny?" Kay said. But she was laughing herself.

"I was just thinking how you wouldn't believe me about Thong-den, and all this time—"

"But I didn't have any idea," she protested. "Not until you and Thongden dug her up."

For some time I sat and stared at the floor in silence. "I still can't believe it," I said at last.

Kay shrugged. "That's reality for you." She was grinning impishly.

Then we both fell into a long, reflective silence, which was broken when Kay suddenly asked me, "You really turned young—like twenty years old?"

I nodded an affirmative.

"What was it like?"

"You mean what was it like being twenty—or what was it like being with Louise?"

"Both. Look—I don't understand any of it. Not about the way time got twisted up, or about this imaginary friend of mine and you—and Thongden. And Superman. I'll admit I feel a little funny. Maybe it's jealousy. But—how far did it go?"

I shook my head in a negative. "Not very far," I assured her. "We kissed. That was it."

"Might it have gone—further?"

Again that negative shake of the head. "I don't think so. We were both a little confused by each other. We sensed the unreality."

Again a long silence. We looked at each other, our gazes alternating with wonder and a kind of new mutual understanding.

"Anything else?" I said at last.

"You said Superman's silence was important," she reminded me.

"I was getting to that. Was there anything else?"

"You can be sure there is. I'll be going on about this for at least a month as questions keep coming to me. But—what about Superman's silence?"

"It was during the carnival ride—when I suddenly realized that I couldn't just call on Superman to save us even though he was supposed to be part of me."

I proceeded to reconstruct the entire event for her as clearly as I could, not only what happened but what I felt, what I thought, and above all the desperate enormous kind of concentration involved. Especially as I experienced it from the side of Superman. So far I hadn't said a word about Thongden's part in the whole affair.

"And what I discovered from that was the real meaning of Superman in my life." I was out of my seat again, pacing the floor as I tried to put together all the scraps of meaning until they finally made sense. "It's as though," I said, "what I was calling on was my highest point of consciousness—a completely focused, undistractable Alvin. That's what it felt like. As though everything that had to do with my being alive was concentrated on the need of that moment." I paused and looked at Kay. "Don't you see—that's what Superman really is. The highest point of individual consciousness. He's totally fixed on a single point. His one defining act—his rescue mission. That's what he does.

He's a being that converges totally, with all his mind and strength and energy, on a single demand arising out of a single moment. He's specialized, you might say, to live entirely in the *now*. You know how adrenaline pulls the whole body together so that all its energy is centered on combating danger? Superman is like that. He's us—when we're truly impermeable, indestructible—totally concentrated. In fact, that's his archetypal reality. It's that very one-pointedness that makes him a kind of cult figure. Because everything big and heroic we ever do is done that way—in the now. You understand? The now is the point of power."

Kay sat quietly, listening carefully.

"Speech is always an afterthought. It has to do with reflection, looking back or looking ahead. The now involves sheer doing. It has nothing to say. That's why Superman was silent." I paused again and looked at Kay. She was listening in rapt attention.

"And that's why," I finished, "you can't have a Superman without a Clark Kent—because no one can live all the time at that level of experience. There has to be a retreat to ordinariness, to self-recollection, to talk and planning and remembering. I think I always knew that, and that's why I wrote my stories the way I did, and why I didn't like it when an editor twisted Superman out of character."

Kay got up suddenly and headed toward the kitchen. I didn't think I had finished. Why was she walking out like that?

"Where are you going?" I called out.

"I thought I'd make some coffee. Maybe just to get back into our Clark Kent mode—get our feet on the ground and feel ordinary for a while?"

"Oh," I said. "Sure."

When she had the coffeemaker working, she came into the living room again. "One more question?"

"Let me guess," I said. "You want to know about Thongden."

"You're getting better at this all the time."

"All right," I said. "What would you say if I told you that Thongden was the one responsible for the collapse of the ride?"

"Thongden? But how was that possible?"

"I have two thoughts about that—at this point. The first is that the *tulpa* finally turned evil. Because in the end, that's why the Tibetans believe a *tulpa* should always be dissolved."

"But that's not the thought you believe," Kay said, watching me closely.

"No—it isn't."

"Well?"

"He warned me in advance about the danger," I said. "Thongden really warned me. And then he brought it about. Because—" I gazed at Kay, "there was something he had to help me discover. I couldn't have done it by myself. I mean—come to grips at last with my own Superman *tulpa* so that I could activate it and then absorb it fully back into myself. If it weren't for that extreme situation he put me into, it never would have happened. A very harsh step—just the sort a Zen master might take. He did it to help me understand."

Kay was silent for a few seconds. "That feels right," she admitted finally. She looked at me. "About Thongden—"

"What about Thongden?"

"Do you think you'll be seeing him again?"

I shrugged. "I don't know. Maybe he wasn't even what he claimed to be. I mean—maybe I created him myself. An independent projection can grow—the same way a book can grow. I've written books that end knowing more than I do. So what can I say? Reality isn't a closed circle with neat endings and everything logically tied together. I haven't a clue about Thongden."

"My own feeling," Kay said, "is that he's through with us. That's what my intuition tells me." Again she fell into a long pause. "Oh—by the way."

"Yes?"

"About Louise . . ."

I looked up at her. "What?"

"I—I'm glad you were—attracted to her."

"You are?"

"Well—she's me, really, isn't she? Me at eighteen right along with you at that age. As though before we ever met—well—we really did know each other."

I took a deep breath. And then I let a big smile break out. "That's a very romantic notion."

"Isn't it?" she said, reaching out and taking my hands in hers. "But it's much more than just a notion, wouldn't you say?"

Afterword

*Rather than living exclusively in disembodied
heavens or "separate realities," we can broaden our
horizons in this world, conceivably, and realize
new kinds of life in contact with more and more
dimensions of the universe. Our further
development, in short, would open the world
we now perceive rather than disengage
us from it.*

—MICHAEL MURPHY[5]

A few days later I dropped in for a talk with Hedy Greene. "I've got an idea for a very different kind of book," I said.

"Oh?"

"About reality."

"How very original."

"And about Superman."

"Interesting mixture. Are you—?"

"No—I'm not going back to writing comics. This is an autobiography. In a way its more than that. Kind of a new form. Maybe I should call it a polybiography."

Hedy sometimes has this arch expression. It's in the way she lifts her eyebrows just a little and then by some feat of physiognomic artistry pulls the end of each one just a little bit down. Anyone who knows her well knows that when she resorts to this expression, she's reading you very accurately.

"You want to tell me something," she said. "But you're afraid you'll make a fool of yourself."

"Let's say I'm sensitive to your skepticism."

She leaned forward, intrigued. "This sounds good," she said. "Why don't you try me?"

It was exactly what I was leading up to. Now that she and I both knew it, I was ready. I started by telling her about Thongden, but only the beginning part. I took it as far as the moment when he exited my kitchen and went trundling off on his bicycle, presumably all the way back to Manhattan by way of the Taconic State Parkway.

"So?" Hedy said.

"You believe it?"

"Why would you make it up?"

"You know about *tulpa*s?"

"I've read about them. Why don't you get on with it?"

That was all the encouragement I needed. I jumped in and proceeded to tell her the whole story, right up to the Superman rescue at the carnival. It took me the better part of two hours. She never once interrupted me. When I finished, there was a barrier of silence between us.

"About the carnival," Hedy said after what seemed a long time.

"What about the carnival?"

"There wasn't anything in the papers about it."

"But Kay said—"

"Every morning before my day begins I go through all the news. Everything of major and minor importance gets downloaded to me via the Internet, I need to stay *au courant*. There was no report of any kind about Superman yesterday. Besides, I don't think there ever was a carnival at that end of the Bronx Zoo. It's city property, you know. But we can check." She started to reach for the phone.

"But Kay said—" I began again, feebly.

"Shall I call?"

"My God—was the whole thing just wild imagination, then? Or are we a little—" I couldn't finish the sentence.

Hedy shook her head. "It all sounds very real to me," she commented surprisingly.

"You're calling it 'real'?"

"Maybe a year ago I wouldn't have understood. But I have this client. He's doing a very interesting book on something called 'the phantom limb syndrome.' You know anything about it?"

"Just that an amputee often continues to feel a missing arm or leg."

"Oh—much more than that. An amputated limb can make its presence felt for years. For decades, in fact. It can itch and burn and—yes—predict the weather by the way it feels. Some amputees can even thrust their phantom limbs through walls."

"But how can they know that?"

"They feel it. There's a whole medical literature on the subject. Phantom limbs tend to shorten or grow depending on whether they're used or not."

"How do you use a phantom limb?"

"By moving it. By letting it fuse with an artificial leg. Anyway, when amputees simply leave the thing alone, it shrinks up. It doesn't go away, though. And as soon as they start to think about it and exercise it, it resumes normal stature again. Doesn't that remind you of something?"

I gave her a blank look.

"About your Thongden—how he needed someone to think about him."

"You're not trying to suggest—"

"Look," Hedy said. "I'm no expert. I'm just passing on what my client is telling me. What he's saying is that on some plane, the whole pattern of the missing limb is still present. That would explain a lot, wouldn't it?—that there's somewhere nonlocal where it exists and continues its former life—actually, its past. What my client is claiming is that somewhere, everything that ever happens to us seems to go on—in some kind of field. Just as real as the gravitational field or the electromagnetic field. The place where all our memories reside and maybe even go on exploring new probabilities."

"Hedy," I said, "you're way ahead of me."

"Actually, it makes sense," she insisted. "No one has ever been able to locate memory anywhere in the brain itself. So where is it? Well, maybe not anywhere in the sense of a place, my client says. And you know, it would explain a lot of strange things. In fact, you should read the biologist Rupert Sheldrake. He's written a great deal on the subject. And let me assure you, he's considered quite respectable as a scientist. Also," she added as though she were just really warming up to the subject, "think of the effect all those yoga breathing exercises might have had on you. Very likely they helped you break through the pattern of your own self-resonance—"

"My what?"

"The sense of who and what we are from day to day. Every morning when we wake up out of our dreams, we reconnect with that sense. But what if those exercises shifted the memory field around for you? What if you connected with a past portion of it? And maybe even with a past portion of the person you're closest to. You see what I mean?"

"Hedy," I said, standing up, "you amaze me. I never expected that you'd—"

"That I'd come out of my straitlaced rational cocoon. Me? After all the starry-eyed New Age clients I've had? All these years and you still don't know me."

"But this is different. In a way, you're trying to tell me that somewhere in some noneveryday plane, Superman rescued me from that carnival ride?"

"The Superman you created, remember that. *Your* Superman. You created him out of a need to visualize him for yourself so you could write Superman continuities all those years. It was one of those personal creations that takes on an independent life—like a book, or a great idea. Where did Planck's constant come from? Planck claims he dreamed it. But it led to Einstein, and after that it simply changed the world. Is that real?"

"But what about Thongden, then?"

Hedy laughed. "I would think he's certainly as real as—Alexander Hamilton." Then she smiled at me as though there were something she knew but wasn't about to say. I let it go at that.

I left Hedy's place, took the subway, and got off at 96th and Broadway. I walked back the few blocks to 89th Street to have a look at Thongden's brownstone. I could tell from the people who went in and out that a new family was living there now. Also, there was a protective iron grill that completely covered the front door.

When I got back home that evening after seeing Hedy Greene and visiting Thongden's old place, I walked into the kitchen and saw Kay at the stove with a frying pan. Because of our diets, practically the only thing she ever fried was a special favorite of mine— my own unique exotic dish—sliced chayote squash dipped in olive oil. For a moment, I watched her turning over the slightly charred slices.

"Kay," I said without ceremony, "where did you read that article about Superman rescuing people at that carnival?"

She didn't look up. "Where? In the newspaper. I told you."

"What newspaper?"

"I don't know. On a plane papers come from all over. I didn't really notice. Maybe the *Calgary Herald*. More likely the *New York Times*. It wasn't my paper, anyway."

"Oh?"

"I mean, I borrowed it from the young man in the seat next to me." She took the pan off the burner for a moment while she reminisced. "You know, I remember thinking how that young man had such nice eyes—like yours. Anyway, I guess he saw me staring at the headline about Superman, so he just smiled at me and handed me the paper. Why?"

"Just wondering," I said quietly. I watched her turning her attention back to the slightly browned chayote slices. The sight was like a quiet assertion of my own secure place in the universe, its gift to me in spite of all its vast and marvelous incomprehensibility. My ordinary, everyday self—now that I understood—was finally the key to everything. It was my entrée to the powers of the universe. And it was also something else. It was the place where the infinite rested on the finite.

Notes

1. Max Freedom Long, *The Secret Science Behind Miracles* (New York: Robert Collier Publications, 1948), pp. 191–192. As I later learned, the accounts by Dr. Brigham and J. A. K. Coombs were well known to many others besides my informant and had even been documented in an odd theosophical work that appeared during the late '40s.
2. Lyall Watson, *The Secret Life of Inanimate Objects* (Rochester, VT: Destiny Books, 1992). The distinguished ethologist, chemist, marine biologist, and anthropologist reveals how complex and animate forms of matter can be produced by mind, suggesting that both matter and mind are aspects of the same thing.
3. Alexandra David-Neel, *Magic and Mystery in Tibet* (New York: Dover Publications, 1971), pp. 314–315.
4. Michael Talbot, *The Holographic Universe* (New York: HarperPerennial, 1991), p. 68 ff. In this broad study of reality as a giant hologram embracing matter and consciousness within a single field, the author describes Stanislav Grof's work with mind-altering drugs that enabled patients to experience the transferring of their consciousnesses into other selves and other species.

5. Michael Murphy, *The Future of the Body* (Los Angeles: Jeremy P. Tarcher, 1992). Murphy theorizes that instead of considering the development of metanormal abilities that carry us to separate worlds, it is preferable to think in terms of a growing wholeness and unity evolving in this world.

A Note to the Reader

An Unlikely Prophet is a book about possibilities. It is meant to help us remember those moments in our lives that have touched the unknown and the unexplainable. In the face of unbending rationality, we need to be reminded to wipe away the dust that so quickly obscures our second vision. While such moments always return we may gradually lose the capacity to see them.

It seems to work that way. It's part of our pattern. It certainly happened to me.

Perhaps now, while the effect of this little book is still fresh in your thoughts, you feel that you won't need such reminders. Perhaps you feel that now you're tightly tuned to the unexpected. But that won't last very long unless you make a *conscious* decision to turn that sensitivity into something permanent.

Let this book be your reminder. Keep it nearby. Carry it with you. Place it where you will see it when you look up from your work or as you walk through your house.

The mind is a great multiplier. If the presence of this book can help maintain your openness to all that is possible, you may begin to notice the daily traces of something out there of which you have never been fully aware. Indeed, you may experience the presence of the marvelous in very direct and surprising ways—if only you will give yourself the license to walk the Path without Form.

—ALVIN SCHWARTZ

About the Author

Alvin Schwartz began his writing career while still in high school during the Little Magazine movement of the 1930s. During his attendance at City College of New York and the University of Chicago, he got to know and was influenced by William Carlos Williams, Gertrude Stein, and other literary luminaries of the day.

He began writing comics for *Fairy Tale Parade* in 1939 and went on to write his first Batman story in 1942 and his first Batman and Superman newspaper strips in 1944. He wrote most of DC Comics's newspaper strips between 1944 and 1952, the Golden Age of Comics, ending his comic writing days with his creation of Bizarro in 1957—his own effort at deconstructing Superman. In 1948, he published his first novel, *The Blowtop,* described by the *New York Times* as the first conscious existentialist novel in America and regarded as one of the first beat novels, having sparked a whole range of subsequent efforts by such writers as Allen Ginsberg and Jack Kerouac.

Winner of the prestigious Canada Council award, Mr. Schwartz has also authored three pseudonymous novels for Arco Press, scripted two feature films, and wrote and researched some thirty docudramas for the National Film Board of Canada.